READING
AND NATIONAL
SOCIALISM

PREFATORY NOTE

The ensuing readings are presented to encourage the student to clarify his thinking on social philosophy. He will accordingly need to determine whether the readings contain a more or less coherent body of ideas which constitutes a social philosophy. He will also need to raise the more far-reaching question whether the ideas are acceptable. To arrive at any satisfactory answer to this latter question, he will necessarily have to compare the ideas of fascism and their practical meanings with the alternatives, real and ideal, that are the substance of live philosophical issues.

CONTENTS

The Doctrine of Fascism
by Benito Mussolini

The Political Doctrine of Fascism
by Alfredo Rocco

The Philosophic Basis of Fascism
by Giovanni Gentile

National Socialism
by Raymond E. Murphy, Francis B. Stevens, Howard Trivers, Joseph M. Roland

National-Socialism and Medicine
by Dr. F. Hamburger

Selected Bibliography

THE DOCTRINE OF FASCISM

ToC

by
BENITO MUSSOLINI
From the ENCYCLOPEDIA ITALIANA. Vol. XIV

The English translation of the "Fundamental Ideas" is by Mr. I.S. Munro, reprinted by his kind permission from "Fascism to World-Power" (Alexander Maclehose, London, 1933).

FUNDAMENTAL IDEAS.
1. Philosophic Conception.

Like every concrete political conception, Fascism is thought and action. It is action with an inherent doctrine which, arising out of a given system of historic forces, is inserted in it and works on it from within. It has therefore a form co-related to the contingencies of time and place; but it has at the same time an ideal content which elevates it into a formula of truth in the higher region of the history of thought.

There is no way of exercising a spiritual influence on the things of the world by means of a human will-power commanding the wills of others, without first having a clear conception of the particular and transient reality on which the will-power must act, and without also having a clear conception of the universal and permanent reality in which the particular and transient reality has its life and being. To know men we must have a knowledge of man; and to have a knowledge of man we must know the reality of things and their laws.

There can be no conception of a State which is not fundamentally a conception of Life. It is a philosophy or intuition, a system of ideas which evolves itself into a system of logical contraction, or which concentrates itself in a vision or in a faith, but which is always, at least virtually, an organic conception of the world.

2. Spiritualised Conception.

Fascism would therefore not be understood in many of its manifestations (as, for example, in its organisations of the Party, its system of education, its discipline) were it not considered in the light of its general view of life. A spiritualised view.

To Fascism the world is not this material world which appears on the surface, in which man is an individual separated from all other men, standing by himself and subject to a natural law which instinctively impels him to lead a life of momentary and egoistic pleasure. In Fascism man is an individual who is the nation and the country. He is this by a moral law which embraces and binds together individuals and generations in an established tradition and mission, a moral law which suppresses the instinct to lead a life confined to a brief cycle of pleasure in order, instead, to replace it within the orbit of duty in a superior conception of life, free from the limits of time and space a life in which the individual by self-abnegation and by the sacrifice of his particular interests, even by death, realises the entirely spiritual existence in which his value as a man consists.

3. Positive Conception of Life as a Struggle.

It is therefore a spiritual conception, itself also a result of the general reaction of the Century against the languid and materialistic positivism of the Eighteenth Century. Anti-positivist, but positive: neither sceptical nor agnostic, neither pessimistic nor passively optimistic, as are in general the doctrines (all of them negative) which place the centre of life outside of man, who by his free will can and should create his own world for himself.

Fascism wants a man to be active and to be absorbed in action with all his energies; it wants him to have a manly consciousness of the difficulties that exist and to be ready to face them. It conceives life as a struggle, thinking that it is the duty of man to conquer that life which is really worthy of him: creating in the first place within himself the (physical, moral, intellectual) instrument with which to build it.

As for the individual, so for the nation, so for mankind. Hence the high value of culture in all its forms (art, religion, science) and the supreme importance of education. Hence also the essential value of labour, with which man conquers nature and creates the human world (economic, political, moral, intellectual).

4. Ethical Conception.

This positive conception of life is evidently an ethical conception. And it comprises the whole reality as well as the human activity which domineers it. No action is to be removed from the moral sense; nothing is to be in the world that is divested of the importance which belongs to it in respect of moral aims. Life, therefore, as the Fascist conceives it, is serious, austere, religious; entirely balanced in a world sustained by the moral and responsible forces of the spirit. The Fascist disdains the "easy" life.

5. Religious Conception.

Fascism is a religious conception in which man is considered to be in the powerful grip of a superior law, with an objective will which transcends the particular individual and elevates him into a fully conscious member of a spiritual society. Anyone who has stopped short at the mere consideration of opportunism in the religious policy of the Fascist Regime, has failed to understand that Fascism, besides being a system of government, is also a system of thought.

6. Historical and Realist Conception.

Fascism is an historical conception in which man could not be what he is without being a factor in the spiritual process to which he contributes, either in the family sphere or in the social sphere, in the nation or in history in general to which all nations contribute. Hence is derived the great importance of tradition in the records, language, customs and rules of human society. Man without a part in history is nothing.

For this reason Fascism is opposed to all the abstractions of an individualistic character based upon materialism typical of the Eighteenth Century; and it is opposed to all the Jacobin innovations and utopias. It does not believe in the possibility of "happiness" on earth as conceived by the literature of the economists of the Seventeenth Century; it therefore spurns all the teleological conceptions of final causes through which, at a given period of history, a final systematisation of the human race would take place. Such theories only mean placing oneself outside real history and life, which is a continual ebb and flow and process of realisations.

Politically speaking, Fascism aims at being a realistic doctrine; in its practice it aspired to solve only the problems which present themselves of their own accord in the process of history, and which of themselves find or suggest their own solution. To have the effect of action among men, it is necessary to enter into the process of reality and to master the forces actually at work.

7. The Individual and Liberty.

Anti-individualistic, the Fascist conception is for the State; it is for the individual only in so far as he coincides with the State, universal consciousness and will of man in his historic existence. It is opposed to the classic Liberalism which arose out of the need of reaction against absolutism, and had accomplished its mission in history when the State itself had become transformed in the popular will and consciousness.

Liberalism denied the State in the interests of the particular individual; Fascism reaffirms the State as the only true expression of the individual.

And if liberty is to be the attribute of the real man, and not of the scarecrow invented by the individualistic Liberalism, then Fascism is for liberty. It is for the only kind of liberty that is serious—the liberty of the State and of the individual in the State. Because, for the Fascist, all is comprised in the State and nothing spiritual or human exists—much less has any value—outside the State. In this respect Fascism is a totalising concept, and the Fascist State—the unification and synthesis of every value—interprets, develops and potentiates the whole life of the people.

8. Conception of a Corporate State.

No individuals nor groups (political parties, associations, labour unions, classes) outside the State. For this reason Fascism is opposed to Socialism, which clings rigidly to class war in the historic evolution and ignores the unity of the State which moulds the classes into a single, moral and economic reality. In the same way Fascism is opposed to the unions of the labouring classes. But within the orbit of the State with ordinative functions, the real needs, which give rise to the Socialist movement and to the forming of labour unions, are emphatically recognised by Fascism and are given their full expression in the Corporative System, which conciliates every interest in the unity of the State.

9. Democracy.

Individuals form classes according to categories of interests. They are associated according to differentiated economical activities which have a common interest: but first and foremost they form the State. The State is not merely either the numbers or the sum of individuals forming the majority of a people. Fascism for this reason is opposed to the democracy which identifies peoples with the greatest number of individuals and reduces them to a majority level. But if people are conceived, as they should be, qualitatively and not quantitatively, then Fascism is democracy in its purest form. The qualitative conception is the most coherent and truest form and is therefore the most moral, because it sees a people realised in the consciousness and will of the few or even of one only; an ideal which moves to its realisation in the consciousness and will of all. By "all" is meant all who derive their justification as a nation, ethnically speaking, from their nature and history, and who follow the same line of spiritual formation and development as one single will and consciousness—not as a race nor as a geographically determined region, but as a progeny that is rather the outcome of a history which perpetuates itself; a multitude unified by an idea embodied in the will to have power and to exist, conscious of itself and of its personality.

10. Conception of the State.

This higher personality is truly the nation, inasmuch as it is the State. The nation does not beget the State, according to the decrepit nationalistic concept which was used as a basis for the publicists of the national States in the Nineteenth Century. On the contrary, the nation is created by the State, which gives the people, conscious of their own moral unity, the will, and thereby an effective existence. The right of a nation to its independence is derived not from a literary and ideal consciousness of its own existence, much less from a *de facto* situation more or less inert and unconscious, but from an active consciousness, from an active political will disposed to demonstrate in its right; that is to say, a kind of State already in its pride (*in fieri*). The State, in fact, as a universal ethical will, is the creator of right.

11. Dynamic Reality.

The nation as a State is an ethical reality which exists and lives in measure as it develops. A standstill is its death. Therefore the State is not only the authority which governs and which gives the forms of law and the worth of the spiritual life to the individual wills, but it is also the power which gives effect to its will in foreign matters, causing it to be recognised and respected by demonstrating through facts the universality of all the manifestations necessary for its development. Hence it is organization as well as expansion, and it may be thereby considered, at least virtually, equal to the very nature of the human will, which in its evolution recognises no barriers, and which realises itself by proving its infinity.

12. The Rôle of the State.

The Fascist State, the highest and the most powerful form of personality is a force, but a spiritual one. It reassumes all the forms of the moral and intellectual life of man. It cannot, therefore, be limited to a simple function of order and of safeguarding, as was contended by Liberalism. It is not a simple mechanism which limits the sphere of the presumed individual liberties. It is an internal form and rule, a discipline of the entire person: it penetrates the will as well as the intelligence. Its principle, a central inspiration of the living human personality in the civil community, descends into the depths and settles in the heart of the man of action as well as the thinker, of the artist as well as of the scientist; the soul of our soul.

13. Discipline and Authority.

Fascism, in short, is not only a lawgiver and the founder of institutions, but an educator and a promoter of the spiritual life. It aims to rebuild not the forms of human life, but its content, the man, the character, the faith. And for this end it exacts discipline and an authority which descend into and dominates the interior of the spirit without opposition. Its emblem, therefore, is the lictorian *fasces*, symbol of unity, of force and of justice.

POLITICAL AND SOCIAL DOCTRINE
1. Origins of the Doctrine.

When, in the now distant March of 1919, I summoned a meeting at Milan, through the columns of the *Popolo d'Italia*, of those who had supported and endured the war and who had followed me since the constitution of the *fasci* or Revolutionary Action in January 1915, there was no specific doctrinal plan in my mind. I had the experience of one only doctrine—that of Socialism from 1903-04 to the winter of 1914 about a decade—but I made it first in the ranks and later as a leader and it was never an experience in theory. My doctrine, even during that period, was a doctrine of action. A universally accepted doctrine of Socialism had not existed since 1915 when the revisionist movement started in Germany, under the leadership of Bernstein. Against this, in the swing of tendencies, a left revolutionary movement began to take shape, but in Italy it never went further than the "field of phrases," whereas in Russian Socialistic circles it became the prelude of Bolscevism. "Reformism," "revolutionarism," "centrism," this is a terminology of which even the echoes are now spent—but in the great river of Fascism are currents which flowed from Sorel, from Peguy, from Lagardelle and the "Mouvement Socialiste," from Italian syndicalists which were legion between 1904 and 1914, and sounded a new note in Italian Socialist circles (weakened then by the betrayal of Giolitti) through Olivetti's *Pagine Libere*, Orano's *La Lupa* and Enrico Leone's *Divenire Sociale*.

After the War, in 1919, Socialism was already dead as a doctrine: it existed only as a grudge. In Italy especially, it had one only possibility of action: reprisals against those who had wanted the War and must now pay its penalty. The *Popolo d'Italia* carried as sub-title "daily of ex-service men and producers," and the word producers was already then the expression of a turn of mind. Fascism was not the nursling of a doctrine previously worked out at a desk; it was born of the need for action and it was action. It was not a party, in fact during the first two years, it was an anti-party and a movement.

The name I gave the organisation fixed its character. Yet whoever should read the now crumpled sheets with the minutes of the meeting at which the Italian "Fasci di Combattimento" were constituted, would fail to discover a doctrine, but would find a series of ideas, of anticipations, of hints which, liberated from the inevitable strangleholds of contingencies, were destined after some years to develop into doctrinal conceptions. Through them Fascism became a political doctrine to itself, different, by comparison, to all others whether contemporary or of the past.

I said then, "If the bourgeoisie think we are ready to act as lightning-conductors, they are mistaken. We must go towards labour. We wish to train the working classes to directive functions. We wish to convince them that it is not easy to manage Industry or Trade: we shall fight the technique and the spirit of the rearguard. When the succession of the regime is open, we must not lack the fighting spirit. We must rush and if the present regime be overcome, it is we who must fill its place. The claim to succession belongs to us, because it was we who forced the country into War and we who led her to victory. The present political representation cannot suffice: we must have a direct representation of all interest. Against this programme one might say it is a return to corporations. But that does not matter. Therefore I should like this assembly to accept the claims put in by national syndicalism from an economic standpoint...."

Is it not strange that the word corporations should have been uttered at the first meeting of Piazza San Sepolcro, when one considers that, in the course of the Revolution, it came to express one of the social and legislative creations at the very foundations of the regime?

2. Development.

The years which preceded the March on Rome were years in which the necessity of action did not permit complete doctrinal investigations or elaborations. The battle was raging in the towns and villages. There were discussions, but what was more important and sacred—there was death. Men knew how to die. The doctrine—all complete and formed, with divisions into chapters, paragraphs, and accompanying elucubrations—might be missing; but there was something more decided to replace it, there was faith.

Notwithstanding, whoever remembers with the aid of books and speeches, whoever could search through them and select, would find that the fundamental principles were laid down whilst the battle raged. It was really in those years that the Fascist idea armed itself, became refined and proceeded towards organisation: the problems of the individual and of the State, the problems of authority and of liberty, the political and social problems, especially national; the fight against the liberal, democratic, socialistic and popular doctrines, was carried out together with the "punitive expeditions."

But as a "system" was lacking, our adversaries in bad faith, denied to Fascism any capacity to produce a doctrine, though that doctrine was growing tumultuously, at first under the aspect of violent and dogmatic negation, as happens to all newly-born ideas, and later under the positive aspect of construction which was successively realised, in the years 1926-27-28 through the laws and institutions of the regime. Fascism today stands clearly defined not only as a regime, but also as a doctrine. This word doctrine should be interpreted in the sense that Fascism, to-day, when passing criticism on itself and others, has its own point of view and its own point of reference, and therefore also its own orientation when facing those problems which beset the world in the spirit and in the matter.

3. Against Pacifism: War and Life as a Duty.

As far as the general future and development of humanity is concerned, and apart from any mere consideration of current politics, Fascism above all does not believe either in the possibility or utility of universal peace. It therefore rejects the pacifism which masks surrender and cowardice. War alone brings all human energies to their highest tension and sets a seal of nobility on the peoples who have the virtue to face it. All other tests are but substitutes which never make a man face himself in the alternative of life or death. A doctrine which has its starting-point at the prejudicial postulate of peace is therefore extraneous to Fascism.

In the same way all international creations (which, as history demonstrates, can be blown to the winds when sentimental, ideal and practical elements storm the heart of a people) are also extraneous to the spirit of Fascism—even if such international creations are accepted for whatever utility they may have in any determined political situation.

Fascism also transports this anti-pacifist spirit into the life of individuals. The proud *squadrista* motto "*me ne frego*" ("I don't give a damn") scrawled on the bandages of the wounded is an act of philosophy—not only stoic. It is a summary of a doctrine not only political: it is an education in strife and an acceptance of the risks which it carried: it is a new style of Italian life. It is thus that the Fascist loves and accepts life, ignores and disdains suicide; understands life as a duty, a lifting up, a conquest; something to be filled in and sustained on a high plane; a thing that has to be lived through for its own sake, but above all for the sake of others near and far, present and future.

4. The Demographic Policy and the "Neighbour."

The "demographic" policy of the regime is the result of these premises. The Fascist also loves his neighbour, but "neighbour" is not for him a vague and undefinable word: love for his neighbour does not prevent necessary educational severities. Fascism rejects professions of universal affection and, though living in the community of civilised peoples, it watches them and looks at them diffidently. It follows them in their state of mind and in the transformation of their interests, but it does not allow itself to be deceived by fallacious and mutable appearances.

5. Against Historical Materialism and Class-Struggle.

Through this conception of life Fascism becomes the emphatic negation of that doctrine which constituted the basis of the so-called scientific Socialism or Marxism: the doctrine of historical materialism, according to which the story of human civilisation is to be explained only by the conflict of interests between the various social groups and by the change of the means and instruments of production.

That the economic vicissitudes—discovery of prime or raw materials, new methods of labour, scientific inventions—have their particular importance, is denied by none, but that they suffice to explain human history, excluding other factors from it, is absurd: Fascism still believes in sanctity and in heroism, that is to say in acts in which no economic motive, immediate or remote, operates.

Fascism having denied historical materialism, by which men are only puppets in history, appearing and disappearing on the surface of the tides while in the depths the real directive forces act and labour, it also denies the immutable and irreparable class warfare, which is the natural filiation of such an economistic conception of history: and it denies above all that class warfare is the preponderating agent of social transformation.

Being defeated on these two capital points of its doctrine, nothing remains of Socialism save the sentimental aspiration—as old as humanity—to achieve a community of social life in which the sufferings and hardships of the humblest classes are alleviated. But here Fascism repudiates the concept of an economic "happiness" which is to be—at a given moment in the evolution of economy—socialistically and almost automatically realised by assuring to all the maximum of well-being.

Fascism denies the possibilities of the materialistic concept of "happiness"—it leaves that to the economists of the first half of the Seventeenth Century; that is, it denies the equation "well-being-happiness," which reduces man to the state of the animals, mindful of only one thing—that of being fed and fattened; reduced, in fact, to a pure and simple vegetative existence.

6. Against Democratic Ideologies.

After disposing of Socialism, Fascism opens a breach on the whole complex of the democratic ideologies, and repudiates them in their theoretic premises as well as in their practical application or instrumentation. Fascism denies that numbers, by the mere fact of being numbers, can direct human society; it denies that these numbers can govern by means of periodical consultations; it affirms also the fertilising, beneficent and unassailable inequality of men, who cannot be levelled through an extrinsic and mechanical process such as universal suffrage.

Regimes can be called democratic which, from time to time, give the people the illusion of being sovereign, whereas the real and effective sovereignty exists in other, and very often secret and irresponsible forces.

Democracy is a regime without a king, but very often with many kings, far more exclusive, tyrannical and ruinous than a single king, even if he be a tyrant. This explains why Fascism which, for contingent reasons, had assumed a republican tendency before 1922, renounced it previous to the March on Rome, with the conviction that the political constitution of a State is not nowadays a supreme question; and that, if the examples of past and present monarchies and past and present republics are studied, the result is that neither monarchies nor republics are to be judged under the assumption of eternity, but that they merely represent forms in which the extrinsic political evolution takes shape as well as the history, the tradition and the psychology of a given country.

Consequently, Fascism glides over the antithesis between monarchy and republic, on which democraticism wasted time, blaming the former for all social shortcomings and exalting the latter as a regime of perfection. We have now seen that there are republics which may be profoundly absolutist and reactionary, and monarchies which welcome the most venturesome social and political experiments.

7. Untruths of Democracy.

"Reason and science" says Renan (who had certain pre-fascist enlightenments) in one of his philosophical meditations, "are products of mankind, but to seek reason directly for the people and through the people is a chimera. It is not necessary for the existence of reason that everybody should know it. In any case if this initiation were to be brought about it could not be through low-class democracy, which seems to lead rather to the extinction of every difficult culture and of every great discipline. The principle that society exists only for the welfare and liberty of individuals composing it, does not seem to conform with the plans of nature: plans in which the species only is taken into consideration and the individual appears sacrificed. It is strongly to be feared that the last word of democracy thus understood (I hasten to add that it can also be differently understood) would be a social state in which a degenerated mass would have no preoccupation other than that of enjoying the ignoble pleasures of the vulgar person."

Thus Renan. In Democracy Fascism rejects the absurd conventional falsehood of political equality, the habit of collective responsibility and the myth of indefinite progress and happiness.

But if there be a different understanding of Democracy if, in other words, Democracy can also signify to not push the people back as far as the margins of the State, then Fascism may well have been defined by the present writer as "an organised, centralised, authoritarian Democracy."

8. Against Liberal Doctrines.

As regards the Liberal doctrines, the attitude of Fascism is one of absolute opposition both in the political and in the economical field. There is no need to exaggerate the importance of Liberalism in the last century—simply for the sake of present-day polemics— and to transform one of the numerous doctrines unfolded in that last century into a religion of humanity for all times, present and future. Liberalism did not flourish for more than a period of fifteen years. It was born in 1830 from the reaction to the Holy Alliance which attempted to set Europe back to the period which preceeded '89 and had its years of splendour in 1848, when also Pius IX was a Liberal. Its decadence began immediately afterwards. If 1848 was a year of light and poesy, 1849 was a year of weakness and tragedy. The Roman Republic was killed by another Republic, the French Republic. In the same year Marx issued his famous manifesto of Communism. In 1851 Napoleon III made his anti-Liberal *coup d'état* and reigned over France until 1870. He was overthrown by a popular movement, following one of the greatest defeats registered in history. The victor was Bismarck, who always ignored the religion of liberty and its prophets. It is symptomatic that a people of high civilisation like the Germans completely ignored the religion of liberty throughout the whole Nineteenth Century—with but one parenthesis, represented by that which was called "the ridiculous parliament of Frankfurt" which lasted one season. Germany realised its national unity outside of Liberalism, against Liberalism—a doctrine which seemed alien to the German spirit essentially monarchical, since Liberalism is the historical and logical ante-chamber of anarchy.

The three wars of 1864, 1866 and 1870 conducted by "Liberals" like Moltke and Bismarck mark the three stages of German unity. As for Italian unity, Liberalism played a very inferior part in the make-up of Mazzini and Garibaldi, who were not liberals. Without the intervention of the anti-Liberal Napoleon we would not have had Lombardy, and without the help of the anti-Liberal Bismarck at Sadowa and Sedan it is very likely that we would not have got Venice in 1866, or that we would have entered Rome in 1870.

During the period of 1870-1915 the preachers of the new Credo themselves denounced the twilight of their religion; it was beaten in the breach by decadence in literature. It was beaten in the open by decadence in practice. Activism: that is to say, nationalism, futurism. Fascism.

The "Liberal Century" after having accumulated an infinity of Gordian knots, sought to cut them in the hecatomb of the World War. Never did any religion impose such a terrible sacrifice. Have the gods of Liberalism slaked their blood-thirst?

Liberalism is now on the point of closing the doors of its deserted temples because nations feel that its agnosticism in the economic field and its indifference in political and moral matters, causes, as it has already caused, the sure ruin of States. That is why all the political experiences of the contemporary world are anti-Liberal, and it is supremely silly to seek to classify them as things outside of history—as if history were a hunting ground reserved to Liberalism and its professors; as if Liberalism were the last and incomparable word of civilisation.

9. Fascism Does Not Turn Back.

The Fascist negation of Socialism, of Democracy, of Liberalism, should not lead one to believe that Fascism wishes to push the world back to where it was before 1879, the date accepted as the opening year of the demo-Liberal century. One cannot turn back. The Fascist doctrine has not chosen De Maistre for its prophet. Monarchical absolutism is a thing of the past, and so is the worship of church power. Feudal privileges and divisions into impenetrable castes with no connection between them, are also "have beens." The conception of Fascist authority has nothing in common with the Police. A party that totally rules a nation is a new chapter in history. References and comparisons are not possible. From the ruins of the socialist, liberal and democratic doctrines, Fascism picks those elements that still have a living value; keeps those that might be termed "facts acquired by history," and rejects the rest: namely the conception of a doctrine good for all times and all people.

Admitting that the Nineteenth Century was the Century of Socialism, Liberalism and Democracy, it is not said that the Twentieth century must also be the century of Socialism, of Liberalism, of Democracy. Political doctrines pass on, but peoples remain. One may now think that this will be the century of authority, the century of the "right wing" the century of Fascism. If the Nineteenth Century was the century of the individual (liberalism signifies individualism) one may think that this will be the century of "collectivism," the century of the State. It is perfectly logical that a new doctrine should utilise the vital elements of other doctrines. No doctrine was ever born entirely new and shining, never seen before. No doctrine can boast of absolute "originality." Each doctrine is bound historically to doctrines which went before, to doctrines yet to come. Thus the scientific Socialism of Marx is bound to the Utopian Socialism of Fourier, of Owen, of Saint-Simon; thus the Liberalism of 1800 is linked with the movement of 1700. Thus Democratic doctrines are bound to the Encyclopaedists. Each doctrine tends to direct human activity towards a definite object; but the activity of man reacts upon the doctrine, transforms it and adapts it to new requirements, or overcomes it. Doctrine therefore should be an act of life and not an academy of words. In this lie the pragmatic veins of Fascism, its will to power, its will to be, its position with regard to "violence" and its value.

10. The Value and Mission of the State.

The capital point of the Fascist doctrine is the conception of the State, its essence, the work to be accomplished, its final aims. In the conception of Fascism, the State is an absolute before which individuals and groups are relative. Individuals and groups are "conceivable" inasmuch as they are in the State. The Liberal State does not direct the movement and the material and spiritual evolution of collectivity, but limits itself to recording the results; the Fascist State has its conscious conviction, a will of its own, and for this reason it is called an "ethical" State.

In 1929 at the first quinquiennial assembly of the Regime, I said: "In Fascism the State is not a night-watchman, only occupied with the personal safety of the citizens, nor is it an organisation with purely material aims, such as that of assuring a certain well-being and a comparatively easy social cohabitation. A board of directors would be quite sufficient to deal with this. It is not a purely political creation, either, detached from the complex material realities of the life of individuals and of peoples. The State as conceived and enacted by Fascism, is a spiritual and moral fact since it gives concrete form to the political, juridical and economical organisation of the country. Furthermore this organisation as it rises and develops, is a manifestation of the spirit. The State is a safeguard of interior and exterior safety but it is also the keeper and the transmitter of the spirit of the people, as it was elaborated throughout the ages, in its language, customs and beliefs. The State is not only the present, but it is also the past and above all the future. The State, inasmuch as it transcends the short limits of individual lives, represents the immanent conscience of the nation. The forms in which the State expresses itself are subject to changes, but the necessity for the State remains. It is the State which educates the citizens in civic virtues, gives them a consciousness of their mission, presses them towards unity; the State harmonizes their interests through justice, transmits to prosperity the attainments of thoughts, in science, in art, in laws, in the solidarity of mankind. The State leads men from primitive tribal life to that highest expression of human power which is Empire; links up through the centuries the names of those who died to preserve its integrity or to obey its laws; holds up the memory of the leaders who increased its territory, and of the geniuses who cast the light of glory upon it, as an example for future generations to follow. When the conception of the State declines and disintegrating or centrifugal tendencies prevail, whether of individuals or groups, then the national society is about to set."

11. The Unity of the State and the Contradictions of Capitalism.

From 1929 onwards to the present day, the universal, political and economical evolution has still further strengthened the doctrinal positions. The giant who rules is the State. The one who can resolve the dramatic contradictions of capital is the State. What is called the crisis cannot be resolved except by the State and in the State. Where are the ghosts of Jules Simon who, at the dawn of Liberalism, proclaimed that "the State must set to work to make itself useless and prepare its resignation?" Of MacCulloch who, in the second half of the past century, proclaimed that the State must abstain from ruling? What would the Englishman Bentham say today to the continual and inevitably-invoked intervention of the State in the sphere of economics, while, according to his theories, industry should ask no more of the State than to be left in peace? Or the German Humboldt according to whom an "idle" State was the best kind of State? It is true that the second wave of Liberal economists were less extreme than the first, and Adam Smith himself opened the door—if only very cautiously—to let State intervention into the economic field.

If Liberalism signifies the individual—then Fascism signifies the State. But the Fascist State is unique of its kind and is an original creation. It is not reactionary but revolutionary, inasmuch as it anticipates the solution of certain universal problems such as those which are treated elsewhere: 1) in the political sphere, by the subdivisions of parties, in the preponderance of parliamentarism and in the irresponsibilities of assemblies; 2) in the economic sphere, by the functions of trade unions which are becoming constantly more numerous and powerful, whether in the labour or industrial fields, in their conflicts and combinations, and 3) in the moral sphere by the necessity of order, discipline, obedience to those who are the moral dictators of the country. Fascism wants the State to be strong, organic and at the same time supported on a wide popular basis. As part of its task the Fascist State has penetrated the economic field: through the corporative, social and educational institutions which it has created. The presence of the State is felt in the remotest ramifications of the country. And in the State also, all the political, economic and spiritual forces of the nation circulate, mustered in their respective organisations.

A State which stands on the support of millions of individuals who recognise it, who believe in it, who are ready to serve it, is not the tyrannical State of the mediaeval lord. It has nothing in common with the absolutist States before or after '89. The individual in the Fascist State is not annulled but rather multiplied, just as in a regiment a soldier is not diminished, but multiplied by the number of his comrades.

The Fascist State organises the nation, but leaves a sufficient margin afterward to the individual; it has limited the useless or harmful liberties and has preserved the essential ones. The one to judge in this respect is not the individual but the State.

12. The Fascist State and Religion.

The Fascist State is not indifferent to the presence or the fact of religion in general nor to the presence of that particular established religion, which is Italian Catholicism. The State has no theology, but it has morality. In the Fascist State religion is considered as one of the most profound manifestations of the spirit; it is therefore not only respected, but defended and protected. The Fascist State does not create its own "God," as Robespierre wanted to do at a certain moment in the frenzies of the Convention; nor does it vainly endeavour to cancel the idea of God from the mind as Bolschevism tries to do. Fascism respects the God of the ascetics, of the saints and of the heroes. It also respects God as he is conceived and prayed to in the ingenuous and primitive heart of the people.

13. Empire and Discipline.

The Fascist State is a will expressing power and empire. The Roman tradition here becomes an idea of force. In the Fascist doctrine, empire is not only a territorial or a military, or a commercial expression: it is a moral and a spiritual one. An empire can be thought of, for instance, as a nation which directly or indirectly guides other nations—without the need of conquering a single mile of territory. For Fascism, the tendency to empire, that is to say the expansion of nations, is a manifestation of vitality, its contrary (the stay-at-home attitude) is a sign of decadence. Peoples who rise, or who suddenly flourish again, are imperialistic; peoples who die are peoples who abdicate. Fascism is a doctrine which most adequately represents the tendencies, the state of mind of a people like the Italian people, which is rising again after many centuries of abandonment and of foreign servitude.

But empire requires discipline, the coordination of forces, duty and sacrifice. This explains many phases of the practical action of the regime. It explains the aims of many of the forces of the State and the necessary severity against those who would oppose themselves to this spontaneous and irresistible movement of the Italy of the Twentieth century by trying to appeal to the discredited ideologies of the Nineteenth century, which have been repudiated wherever great experiments of political and social transformation have been daringly undertaken.

Never more than at the present moment have the nations felt such a thirst for an authority, for a direction, for order. If every century has its own peculiar doctrine, there are a thousand indications that Fascism is that of the present century. That it is a doctrine of life is shown by the fact that it has created a faith; that the faith has taken possession of the mind is demonstrated by the fact that Fascism has had its Fallen and its martyrs.

Fascism has now attained in the world an universality over all doctrines. Being realised, it represents an epoch in the history of the human mind.

THE POLITICAL DOCTRINE OF FASCISM[1]

by
His Excellency Alfredo Rocco

Premier Mussolini's Endorsement Of Signor Rocco's Speech

The following message was sent by Benito Mussolini, the Premier of Italy, to Signor Rocco after he had delivered his speech at Perugia.
Dear Rocco,

I have just read your magnificent address which I endorse throughout. You have presented in a masterful way the doctrine of Fascism. For Fascism has a doctrine, or, if you will, a particular philosophy with regard to all the questions which beset the human mind today. All Italian Fascists should read your discourse and derive from it both the clear formulation of the basic principles of our program as well as the reasons why Fascism must be systematically, firmly, and rationally inflexible in its uncompromising attitude towards other parties. Thus and only thus can the word become flesh and the ideas be turned into deeds.

Cordial greetings,
Mussolini.

Fascism As Action, As Feeling, and As Thought

Much has been said, and is now being said for or against this complex political and social phenomenon which in the brief period of six years has taken complete hold of Italian life and, spreading beyond the borders of the Kingdom, has made itself felt in varying degrees of intensity throughout the world. But people have been much more eager to extol or to deplore than to understand—which is natural enough in a period of tumultuous fervor and of political passion. The time has not yet arrived for a dispassionate judgment. For even I, who noticed the very first manifestations of this great development, saw its significance from the start and participated directly in its first doings, carefully watching all its early uncertain and changing developments, even I do not feel competent to pass definite judgment. Fascism is so large a part of myself that it would be both arbitrary and absurd for me to try to dissociate my personality from it, to submit it to impartial scrutiny in order to evaluate it coldly and accurately. What can be done, however, and it seldom is attempted, is to make inquiry into the phenomenon which shall not merely consider its fragmentary and adventitious aspects, but strive to get at its inner essence. The undertaking may not be easy, but it is necessary, and no occasion for attempting it is more suitable than the present one afforded me by my friends of Perugia. Suitable it is in time because, at the inauguration of a course of lectures and lessons principally intended to illustrate that old and glorious trend of the life and history of Italy which takes its name from the humble saint of Assisi, it seemed natural to connect it with the greatest achievement of modern Italy, different in so many ways from the Franciscan movement, but united with it by the mighty common current of Italian History. It is suitable as well in place because at Perugia, which witnessed the growth of our religious ideas, of our political doctrines and of our legal science in the course of the most glorious centuries of our cultural history, the mind is properly disposed and almost oriented towards an investigation of this nature.

First of all let us ask ourselves if there is a political doctrine of Fascism; if there is any ideal content in the Fascist state. For in order to link Fascism, both as concept and system, with the history of Italian thought and find therein a place for it, we must first show that it is thought; that it is a doctrine. Many persons are not quite convinced that it is either the one or the other; and I am not referring solely to those men, cultured or uncultured, as the case may be and very numerous everywhere, who can discern in this political innovation nothing except its local and personal aspects, and who know Fascism only as the particular manner of behavior of this or that well-known Fascist, of this or that group of a certain town; who therefore like or dislike the movement on the basis of their likes and dislikes for the individuals who represent it. Nor do I refer to those intelligent, and cultivated persons, very intelligent indeed and very cultivated, who because of their direct or indirect allegiance to the parties that have been dispossessed by the advent of Fascism, have a natural cause of resentment against it and are therefore unable to see, in the blindness of hatred, anything good in it. I am referring rather to those—and there are many in our ranks too—who know Fascism as action and feeling but not yet as thought, who therefore have an intuition but no comprehension of it.

It is true that Fascism is, above all, action and sentiment and that such it must continue to be. Were it otherwise, it could not keep up that immense driving force, that renovating power which it now possesses and would merely be the solitary meditation of a chosen few. Only because it is feeling and sentiment, only because it is the unconscious reawakening of our profound racial instinct, has it the force to stir the soul of the people, and to set free an irresistible current of national will. Only because it is action, and as such actualizes itself in a vast organization and in a huge movement, has it the conditions for determining the historical course of contemporary Italy.

But Fascism is thought as well and it has a theory, which is an essential part of this historical phenomenon, and which is responsible in a great measure for the successes that have been achieved. To the existence of this ideal content of Fascism, to the truth of this Fascist logic we ascribe the fact that though we commit many errors of detail, we very seldom go astray on fundamentals, whereas all the parties of the opposition, deprived as they are of an informing, animating principle, of a unique directing concept, do very often wage their war faultlessly in minor tactics, better trained as they are in parliamentary and journalistic manoeuvres, but they constantly break down on the important issues. Fascism, moreover, considered as action, is a typically Italian phenomenon and acquires a universal validity because of the existence of this coherent and organic doctrine. The originality of Fascism is due in great part to the autonomy of its theoretical principles. For even when, in its external behavior and in its conclusions, it seems identical with other political creeds, in reality it possesses an inner originality due to the new spirit which animates it and to an entirely different theoretical approach.

Common Origins and Common Background of Modern Political Doctrines: From Liberalism to Socialism

Modern political thought remained, until recently, both in Italy and outside of Italy under the absolute control of those doctrines which, proceeding from the Protestant Reformation and developed by the adepts of natural law in the XVII and XVIII centuries, were firmly grounded in the institutions and customs of the English, of the American, and of the French Revolutions. Under different and sometimes clashing forms these doctrines have left a determining imprint upon all theories and actions both social and political, of the XIX and XX centuries down to the rise of Fascism. The common basis of all these doctrines, which stretch from Longuet, from Buchanan, and from Althusen down to Karl Marx, to Wilson and to Lenin is a social and state concept which I shall call mechanical or atomistic.

Society according to this concept is merely a sum total of individuals, a plurality which breaks up into its single components. Therefore the ends of a society, so considered, are nothing more than the ends of the individuals which compose it and for whose sake it exists. An atomistic view of this kind is also necessarily anti-historical, inasmuch as it considers society in its spatial attributes and not in its temporal ones; and because it reduces social life to the existence of a single generation. Society becomes thus a sum of determined individuals, viz., the generation living at a given moment. This doctrine which I call atomistic and which appears to be anti-historical, reveals from under a concealing cloak a strongly materialistic nature. For in its endeavors to isolate the present from the past and the future, it rejects the spiritual inheritance of ideas and sentiments which each generation receives from those preceding and hands down to the following generation thus destroying the unity and the spiritual life itself of human society.

This common basis shows the close logical connection existing between all political doctrines; the substantial solidarity, which unites all the political movements, from Liberalism to Socialism, that until recently have dominated Europe. For these political schools differ from one another in their methods, but all agree as to the ends to be achieved. All of them consider the welfare and happiness of individuals to be the goal of society, itself considered as composed of individuals of the present generation. All of them see in society and in its juridical organization, the state, the mere instrument and means whereby individuals can attain their ends. They differ only in that the methods pursued for the attainment of these ends vary considerably one from the other.

Thus the Liberals insist that the best manner to secure the welfare of the citizens as individuals is to interfere as little as possible with the free development of their activities and that therefore the essential task of the state is merely to coordinate these several liberties in such a way as to guarantee their coexistence. Kant, who was without doubt the most powerful and thorough philosopher of liberalism, said, "man, who is the end, cannot be assumed to have the value of an instrument." And again, "justice, of which the state is the specific organ, is the condition whereby the freedom of each is conditioned upon the freedom of others, according to the general law of liberty."

Having thus defined the task of the state, Liberalism confines itself to the demand of certain guarantees which are to keep the state from overstepping its functions as general coordinator of liberties and from sacrificing the freedom of individuals more than is absolutely necessary for the accomplishment of its purpose. All the efforts are therefore directed to see to it that the ruler, mandatory of all and entrusted with the realization, through and by liberty, of the harmonious happiness of everybody, should never be clothed with undue power. Hence the creation of a system of checks and limitations designed to keep the rulers within bounds; and among these, first and foremost, the principle of the division of powers, contrived as a means for weakening the state in its relation to the individual, by making it impossible for the state ever to appear, in its dealings with citizens, in the full plenitude of sovereign powers; also the principle of the participation of citizens in the lawmaking power, as a means for securing, in behalf of the individual, a direct check on this, the strongest branch, and an indirect check on the entire government of the state. This system of checks and limitations, which goes by the name of constitutional government resulted in a moderate and measured liberalism. The checking power was exercised only by those citizens who were deemed worthy and capable, with the result that a small élite was made to represent legally the entire body politic for whose benefit this régime was instituted.

It was evident, however, that this moderate system, being fundamentally illogical and in contradiction with the very principles from which it proceeded, would soon become the object of serious criticism. For if the object of society and of the state is the welfare of individuals, severally considered, how is it possible to admit that this welfare can be secured by the individuals themselves only through the possibilities of such a liberal régime? The inequalities brought about both by nature and by social organizations are so numerous and so serious, that, for the greater part, individuals abandoned to themselves not only would fail to attain happiness, but would also contribute to the perpetuation of their condition of misery and dejection. The state therefore cannot limit itself to the merely negative function of the defense of liberty. It must become active, in behalf of everybody, for the welfare of the people. It must intervene, when necessary, in order to improve the material, intellectual, and moral conditions of the masses; it must find work for the unemployed, instruct and educate the people, and care for health and hygiene. For if the purpose of society and of the state is the welfare of individuals, and if it is just that these individuals themselves control the attainment of their ends, it becomes difficult to understand why Liberalism should not go the whole distance, why it should see fit to distinguish certain individuals from the rest of the mass, and why the functions of the people should be restricted to the exercise of a mere check. Therefore the state, if it exists for all, must be governed by all, and not by a small minority: if the state is for the people, sovereignty must reside in the people: if all individuals have the right to govern the state, liberty is no longer sufficient; equality must be added: and if sovereignty is vested in the people, the people must wield all sovereignty and not merely a part of it. The power to check and curb the government is not sufficient. The people must be the government. Thus, logically developed, Liberalism leads to Democracy, for Democracy contains the promises of Liberalism but oversteps its limitations in that it makes the action of the state positive, proclaims the equality of all citizens through the dogma of popular sovereignty. Democracy therefore necessarily implies a republican form of government even though at times, for reasons of expediency, it temporarily adjusts itself to a monarchical régime.

Once started on this downward grade of logical deductions it was inevitable that this atomistic theory of state and society should pass on to a more advanced position. Great industrial developments and the existence of a huge mass of working men, as yet badly treated and in a condition of semi-servitude, possibly endurable in a régime of domestic industry, became intolerable after the industrial revolution. Hence a state of affairs which towards the middle of the last century appeared to be both cruel and threatening. It was therefore natural that the following question be raised: "If the state is created for the welfare of its citizens, severally considered, how can it tolerate an economic system which divides the population into a small minority of exploiters, the capitalists, on one side, and an immense multitude of exploited, the working people, on the other?" No! The state must again intervene and give rise to a different and less iniquitous economic organization, by abolishing private property, by assuming direct control of all production, and by organizing it in such a way that the products of labor be distributed solely among those who create them, viz., the working classes. Hence we find Socialism, with its new economic organization of society, abolishing private ownership of capital and of the instruments and means of production, socializing the product, suppressing the extra profit of capital, and turning over to the working class the entire output of the productive processes. It is evident that Socialism contains and surpasses Democracy in the same way that Democracy comprises and surpasses Liberalism, being a more advanced development of the same fundamental concept. Socialism in its turn generates the still more extreme doctrine of Bolshevism which demands the violent suppression of the holders of capital, the dictatorship of the proletariat, as means for a fairer economic organization of society and for the rescue of the laboring classes from capitalistic exploitation.

Thus Liberalism, Democracy, and Socialism, appear to be, as they are in reality, not only the offspring of one and the same theory of government, but also logical derivations one of the other. Logically developed Liberalism leads to Democracy; the logical development of Democracy issues into Socialism. It is true that for many years, and with some justification, Socialism was looked upon as antithetical to Liberalism. But the antithesis is purely relative and breaks down as we approach the common origin and foundation of the two doctrines, for we find that the opposition is one of method, not of purpose. The end is the same for both, viz., the welfare of the individual members of society. The difference lies in the fact that Liberalism would be guided to its goal by liberty, whereas Socialism strives to attain it by the collective organization of production. There is therefore no antithesis nor even a divergence as to the nature and scope of the state and the relation of individuals to society. There is only a difference of evaluation of the means for bringing about these ends and establishing these relations, which difference depends entirely on the different economic conditions which prevailed at the time when the various doctrines were formulated. Liberalism arose and began to thrive in the period of small industry; Socialism grew with the rise of industrialism and of world-wide capitalism. The dissension therefore between these two points of view, or the antithesis, if we wish so to call it, is limited to the economic field. Socialism is at odds with Liberalism only on the question of the organization of production and of the division of wealth. In religious, intellectual, and moral matters it is liberal, as it is liberal and democratic in its politics. Even the anti-liberalism and anti-democracy of Bolshevism are in themselves purely contingent. For Bolshevism is opposed to Liberalism only in so far as the former is revolutionary, not in its socialistic aspect. For if the opposition of the Bolsheviki to liberal and democratic doctrines were to continue, as now seems more and more probable, the result might be a complete break between Bolshevism and Socialism notwithstanding the fact that the ultimate aims of both are identical.

Fascism as an Integral Doctrine of Sociality Antithetical to the Atomism of Liberal, Democratic, and Socialistic Theories

The true antithesis, not to this or that manifestation of the liberal-democratic-socialistic conception of the state but to the concept itself, is to be found in the doctrine of Fascism. For while the disagreement between Liberalism and Democracy, and between Liberalism and Socialism lies in a difference of method, as we have said, the rift between Socialism, Democracy, and Liberalism on one side and Fascism on the other is caused by a difference in concept. As a matter of fact, Fascism never raises the question of methods, using in its political praxis now liberal ways, now democratic means and at times even socialistic devices. This indifference to method often exposes Fascism to the charge of incoherence on the part of superficial observers, who do not see that what counts with us is the end and that therefore even when we employ the same means we act with a radically different spiritual attitude and strive for entirely different results. The Fascist concept then of the nation, of the scope of the state, and of the relations obtaining between society and its individual components, rejects entirely the doctrine which I said proceeded from the theories of natural law developed in the course of the XVI, XVII, and XVIII centuries and which form the basis of the liberal, democratic, and socialistic ideology.

I shall not try here to expound this doctrine but shall limit myself to a brief résumé of its fundamental concepts.

Man—the political animal—according to the definition of Aristotle, lives and must live in society. A human being outside the pale of society is an inconceivable thing—a non-man. Humankind in its entirety lives in social groups that are still, today, very numerous and diverse, varying in importance and organization from the tribes of Central Africa to the great Western Empires. These various societies are fractions of the human species each one of them endowed with a unified organization. And as there is no unique organization of the human species, there is not "one" but there are "several" human societies. Humanity therefore exists solely as a biological concept not as a social one.

Each society on the other hand exists in the unity of both its biological and its social contents. Socially considered it is a fraction of the human species endowed with unity of organization for the attainment of the peculiar ends of the species.

This definition brings out all the elements of the social phenomenon and not merely those relating to the preservation and perpetuation of the species. For man is not solely matter; and the ends of the human species, far from being the materialistic ones we have in common with other animals, are, rather, and predominantly, the spiritual finalities which are peculiar to man and which every form of society strives to attain as well as its stage of social development allows. Thus the organization of every social group is more or less pervaded by the spiritual influxes of: unity of language, of culture, of religion, of tradition, of customs, and in general of feeling and of volition, which are as essential as the material elements: unity of economic interests, of living conditions, and of territory. The definition given above demonstrates another truth, which has been ignored by the political doctrines that for the last four centuries have been the foundations of political systems, viz., that the social concept has a biological aspect, because social groups are fractions of the human species, each one possessing a peculiar organization, a particular rank in the development of civilization with certain needs and appropriate ends, in short, a life which is really its own. If social groups are then fractions of the human species, they must possess the same fundamental traits of the human species, which means that they must be considered as a succession of generations and not as a collection of individuals.

It is evident therefore that as the human species is not the total of the living human beings of the world, so the various social groups which compose it are not the sum of the several individuals which at a given moment belong to it, but rather the infinite series of the past, present, and future generations constituting it. And as the ends of the human species are not those of the several individuals living at a certain moment, being occasionally in direct opposition to them, so the ends of the various social groups are not necessarily those of the individuals that belong to the groups but may even possibly be in conflict with such ends, as one sees clearly whenever the preservation and the development of the species demand the sacrifice of the individual, to wit, in times of war.

Fascism replaces therefore the old atomistic and mechanical state theory which was at the basis of the liberal and democratic doctrines with an organic and historic concept. When I say organic I do not wish to convey the impression that I consider society as an organism after the manner of the so-called "organic theories of the state"; but rather to indicate that the social groups as fractions of the species receive thereby a life and scope which transcend the scope and life of the individuals identifying themselves with the history and finalities of the uninterrupted series of generations. It is irrelevant in this connection to determine whether social groups, considered as fractions of the species, constitute organisms. The important thing is to ascertain that this organic concept of the state gives to society a continuous life over and beyond the existence of the several individuals.

The relations therefore between state and citizens are completely reversed by the Fascist doctrine. Instead of the liberal-democratic formula, "society for the individual," we have, "individuals for society" with this difference however: that while the liberal doctrines eliminated society, Fascism does not submerge the individual in the social group. It subordinates him, but does not eliminate him; the individual as a part of his generation ever remaining an element of society however transient and insignificant he may be. Moreover the development of individuals in each generation, when coordinated and harmonized, conditions the development and prosperity of the entire social unit.

At this juncture the antithesis between the two theories must appear complete and absolute. Liberalism, Democracy, and Socialism look upon social groups as aggregates of living individuals; for Fascism they are the recapitulating unity of the indefinite series of generations. For Liberalism, society has no purposes other than those of the members living at a given moment. For Fascism, society has historical and immanent ends of preservation, expansion, improvement, quite distinct from those of the individuals which at a given moment compose it; so distinct in fact that they may even be in opposition. Hence the necessity, for which the older doctrines make little allowance, of sacrifice, even up to the total immolation of individuals, in behalf of society; hence the true explanation of war, eternal law of mankind, interpreted by the liberal-democratic doctrines as a degenerate absurdity or as a maddened monstrosity.

For Liberalism, society has no life distinct from the life of the individuals, or as the phrase goes: solvitur in singularitates. For Fascism, the life of society overlaps the existence of individuals and projects itself into the succeeding generations through centuries and millennia. Individuals come into being, grow, and die, followed by others, unceasingly; social unity remains always identical to itself. For Liberalism, the individual is the end and society the means; nor is it conceivable that the individual, considered in the dignity of an ultimate finality, be lowered to mere instrumentality. For Fascism, society is the end, individuals the means, and its whole life consists in using individuals as instruments for its social ends. The state therefore guards and protects the welfare and development of individuals not for their exclusive interest, but because of the identity of the needs of individuals with those of society as a whole. We can thus accept and explain institutions and practices, which like the death penalty, are condemned by Liberalism in the name of the preeminence of individualism.

The fundamental problem of society in the old doctrines is the question of the rights of individuals. It may be the right to freedom as the Liberals would have it; or the right to the government of the commonwealth as the Democrats claim it, or the right to economic justice as the Socialists contend; but in every case it is the right of individuals, or groups of individuals (classes). Fascism on the other hand faces squarely the problem of the right of the state and of the duty of individuals. Individual rights are only recognized in so far as they are implied in the rights of the state. In this preeminence of duty we find the highest ethical value of Fascism.

The Problems of Liberty, of Government, and of Social Justice in the Political Doctrine of Fascism

This, however, does not mean that the problems raised by the other schools are ignored by Fascism. It means simply that it faces them and solves them differently, as, for example, the problem of liberty.

There is a Liberal theory of freedom, and there is a Fascist concept of liberty. For we, too, maintain the necessity of safeguarding the conditions that make for the free development of the individual; we, too, believe that the oppression of individual personality can find no place in the modern state. We do not, however, accept a bill of rights which tends to make the individual superior to the state and to empower him to act in opposition to society. Our concept of liberty is that the individual must be allowed to develop his personality in behalf of the state, for these ephemeral and infinitesimal elements of the complex and permanent life of society determine by their normal growth the development of the state. But this individual growth must be normal. A huge and disproportionate development of the individual of classes, would prove as fatal to society as abnormal growths are to living organisms. Freedom therefore is due to the citizen and to classes on condition that they exercise it in the interest of society as a whole and within the limits set by social exigencies, liberty being, like any other individual right, a concession of the state. What I say concerning civil liberties applies to economic freedom as well. Fascism does not look upon the doctrine of economic liberty as an absolute dogma. It does not refer economic problems to individual needs, to individual interest, to individual solutions. On the contrary it considers the economic development, and especially the production of wealth, as an eminently social concern, wealth being for society an essential element of power and prosperity. But Fascism maintains that in the ordinary run of events economic liberty serves the social purposes best; that it is profitable to entrust to individual initiative the task of economic development both as to production and as to distribution; that in the economic world individual ambition is the most effective means for obtaining the best social results with the least effort. Therefore, on the question also of economic liberty the Fascists differ fundamentally from the Liberals; the latter see in liberty a principle, the the Fascists accept it as a method. By the Liberals, freedom is recognized in the interest of the citizens; the Fascists grant it in the interest of society. In other terms, Fascists make of the individual an economic instrument for the advancement of society, an instrument which they use so long as it functions and which they subordinate when no longer serviceable. In this guise Fascism solves the eternal problem of economic freedom and of state interference, considering both as mere methods which may or may not be employed in accordance with the social needs of the moment.

What I have said concerning political and economic Liberalism applies also to Democracy. The latter envisages fundamentally the problem of sovereignty; Fascism does also, but in an entirely different manner. Democracy vests sovereignty in the people, that is to say, in the mass of human beings. Fascism discovers sovereignty to be inherent in society when it is juridically organized as a state. Democracy therefore turns over the government of the state to the multitude of living men that they may use it to further their own interests; Fascism insists that the government be entrusted to men capable of rising above their own private interests and of realizing the aspirations of the social collectivity, considered in its unity and in its relation to the past and future. Fascism therefore not only rejects the dogma of popular sovereignty and substitutes for it that of state sovereignty, but it also proclaims that the great mass of citizens is not a suitable advocate of social interests for the reason that the capacity to ignore individual private interests in favor of the higher demands of society and of history is a very rare gift and the privilege of the chosen few. Natural intelligence and cultural preparation are of great service in such tasks. Still more valuable perhaps is the intuitiveness of rare great minds, their traditionalism and their inherited qualities. This must not however be construed to mean that the masses are not to be allowed to exercise any influence on the life of the state. On the contrary, among peoples with a great history and with noble traditions, even the lowest elements of society possess an instinctive discernment of what is necessary for the welfare of the race, which in moments of great historical crises reveals itself to be almost infallible. It is therefore as wise to afford to this instinct the means of declaring itself as it is judicious to entrust the normal control of the commonwealth to a selected élite.

As for Socialism, the Fascist doctrine frankly recognizes that the problem raised by it as to the relations between capital and labor is a very serious one, perhaps the central one of modern life. What Fascism does not countenance is the collectivistic solution proposed by the Socialists. The chief defect of the socialistic method has been clearly demonstrated by the experience of the last few years. It does not take into account human nature, it is therefore outside of reality, in that it will not recognize that the most powerful spring of human activities lies in individual self-interest and that therefore the elimination from the economic field of this interest results in complete paralysis. The suppression of private ownership of capital carries with it the suppression of capital itself, for capital is formed by savings and no one will want to save, but will rather consume all he makes if he knows he cannot keep and hand down to his heirs the results of his labors. The dispersion of capital means the end of production since capital, no matter who owns it, is always an indispensable tool of production. Collective organization of production is followed therefore by the paralysis of production since, by eliminating from the productive mechanism the incentive of individual interest, the product becomes rarer and more costly. Socialism then, as experience has shown, leads to increase in consumption, to the dispersion of capital and therefore to poverty. Of what avail is it, then, to build a social machine which will more justly distribute wealth if this very wealth is destroyed by the construction of this machine? Socialism committed an irreparable error when it made of private property a matter of justice while in truth it is a problem of social utility. The recognition of individual property rights, then, is a part of the Fascist doctrine not because of its individual bearing but because of its social utility.

We must reject, therefore, the socialistic solution but we cannot allow the problem raised by the Socialists to remain unsolved, not only because justice demands a solution but also because the persistence of this problem in liberal and democratic régimes has been a menace to public order and to the authority of the state. Unlimited and unrestrained class self-defense, evinced by strikes and lockouts, by boycotts and sabotage, leads inevitably to anarchy. The Fascist doctrine, enacting justice among the classes in compliance with a fundamental necessity of modern life, does away with class self-defense, which, like individual self-defense in the days of barbarism, is a source of disorder and of civil war.

Having reduced the problem of these terms, only one solution is possible, the realization of justice among the classes by and through the state. Centuries ago the state, as the specific organ of justice, abolished personal self-defense in individual controversies and substituted for it state justice. The time has now come when class self-defense also must be replaced by state justice. To facilitate the change Fascism has created its own syndicalism. The suppression of class self-defense does not mean the suppression of class defense which is an inalienable necessity of modern economic life. Class organization is a fact which cannot be ignored but it must be controlled, disciplined, and subordinated by the state. The syndicate, instead of being, as formerly, an organ of extra-legal defense, must be turned into an organ of legal defense which will become judicial defense as soon as labor conflicts become a matter of judicial settlement. Fascism therefore has transformed the syndicate, that old revolutionary instrument of syndicalistic socialists, into an instrument of legal defense of the classes both within and without the law courts. This solution may encounter obstacles in its development; the obstacles of malevolence, of suspicion of the untried, of erroneous calculation, etc., but it is destined to triumph even though it must advance through progressive stages.

Historical Value of the Doctrine of Fascism

I might carry this analysis farther but what I have already said is sufficient to show that the rise of a Fascist ideology already gives evidence of an upheaval in the intellectual field as powerful as the change that was brought about in the XVII and XVIII centuries by the rise and diffusion of those doctrines of *ius naturale* which go under the name of "Philosophy of the French Revolution." The philosophy of the French Revolution formulated certain principles, the authority of which, unquestioned for a century and a half, seemed so final that they were given the attribute of immortality. The influence of these principles was so great that they determined the formation of a new culture, of a new civilization. Likewise the fervor of the ideas that go to make up the Fascist doctrine, now in its inception but destined to spread rapidly, will determine the course of a new culture and of a new conception of civil life. The deliverance of the individual from the state carried out in the XVIII century will be followed in the XX century by the rescue of the state from the individual. The period of authority, of social obligations, of "hierarchical" subordination will succeed the period of individualism, of state feebleness, of insubordination.

This innovating trend is not and cannot be a return to the Middle Ages. It is a common but an erroneous belief that the movement, started by the Reformation and heightened by the French Revolution, was directed against mediaeval ideas and institutions. Rather than as a negation, this movement should be looked upon as the development and fulfillment of the doctrines and practices of the Middle Ages. Socially and politically considered the Middle Ages wrought disintegration and anarchy; they were characterized by the gradual weakening and ultimate extinction of the state, embodied in the Roman Empire, driven first to the East, then back to France, thence to Germany, a shadow of its former self; they were marked by the steady advance of the forces of usurpation, destructive of the state and reciprocally obnoxious; they bore the imprints of a triumphant particularism. Therefore the individualistic and anti-social movement of the XVII and XVIII centuries was not directed against the Middle Ages, but rather against the restoration of the state by great national monarchies. If this movement destroyed mediaeval institutions that had survived the Middle Ages and had been grafted upon the new states, it was in consequence of the struggle primarily waged against the state. The spirit of the movement was decidedly mediaeval. The novelty consisted in the social surroundings in which it operated and in its relation to new economic developments. The individualism of the feudal lords, the particularism of the cities and of the corporations had been replaced by the individualism and the particularism of the bourgeoisie and of the popular classes.

The Fascist ideology cannot therefore look back to the Middle Ages, of which it is a complete negation. The Middle Ages spell disintegration; Fascism is nothing if not sociality. It is if anything the beginning of the end of the Middle Ages prolonged four centuries beyond the end ordinarily set for them and revived by the social democratic anarchy of the past thirty years. If Fascism can be said to look back at all it is rather in the direction of ancient Rome whose social and political traditions at the distance of fifteen centuries are being revived by Fascist Italy.

I am fully aware that the value of Fascism, as an intellectual movement, baffles the minds of many of its followers and supporters and is denied outright by its enemies. There is no malice in this denial, as I see it, but rather an incapacity to comprehend. The liberal-democratic-socialistic ideology has so completely and for so long a time dominated Italian culture that in the minds of the majority of people trained by it, it has assumed the value of an absolute truth, almost the authority of a natural law. Every faculty of self-criticism is suppressed in the minds and this suppression entails an incapacity for understanding that time alone can change. It will be advisable therefore to rely mainly upon the new generations and in general upon persons whose culture is not already fixed. This difficulty to comprehend on the part of those who have been thoroughly grounded by a different preparation in the political and social sciences explains in part why Fascism has not been wholly successful with the intellectual classes and with mature minds, and why on the other hand it has been very successful with young people, with women, in rural districts, and among men of action unencumbered by a fixed and set social and political education. Fascism moreover, as a cultural movement, is just now taking its first steps. As in the case with all great movements, action regularly outstrips thought. It was thus at the time of the Protestant Reformation and of the individualistic reaction of the XVII and XVIII centuries. The English revolution occurred when the doctrines of natural law were coming into being and the theoretical development of the liberal and democratic theories followed the French Revolution.

At this point it will not be very difficult to assign a fitting place in history to this great trend of thought which is called Fascism and which, in spite of the initial difficulties, already gives clear indication of the magnitude of its developments.

The liberal-democratic speculation both in its origin and in the manner of its development appears to be essentially a non-Italian formation. Its connection with the Middle Ages already shows it to be foreign to the Latin mind, the mediaeval disintegration being the result of the triumph of Germanic individualism over the political mentality of the Romans. The barbarians, boring from within and hacking from without, pulled down the great political structure raised by Latin genius and put nothing in its place. Anarchy lasted eight centuries during which time only one institution survived and that a Roman one—the Catholic Church. But, as soon as the laborious process of reconstruction was started with the constitution of the great national states backed by the Roman Church the Protestant Reformation set in followed by the individualistic currents of the XVII and XVIII centuries, and the process of disintegration was started anew. This anti-state tendency was the expression of the Germanic spirit and it therefore became predominant among the Germanic peoples and wherever Germanism had left a deep imprint even if afterward superficially covered by a veneer of Latin culture. It is true that Marsilius from Padua is an Italian writing for Ludwig the Bavarian, but the other writers who in the XIV century appear as forerunners of the liberal doctrines are not Italians: Occam and Wycliff are English; Oresme is French. Among the advocates of individualism in the XVI century who prepared the way for the triumph of the doctrines of natural law in the subsequent centuries, Hotman and Languet are French, Buchanan is Scotch. Of the great authorities of natural law, Grotius and Spinosa are Dutch; Locke is English; l'Abbé de St. Pierre, Montesquieu, d'Argenson, Voltaire, Rousseau, Diderot and the encyclopaedists are French; Althusius, Pufendorf, Kant, Fichte are German.

Italy took no part in the rise and development of the doctrines of natural law. Only in the XIX century did she evince a tardy interest in these doctrines, just as she tardily contributed to them at the close of the XVIII century through the works of Beccaria and Filangeri.

While therefore in other countries such as France, England, Germany, and Holland, the general tradition in the social and political sciences worked in behalf of anti-state individualism, and therefore of liberal and democratic doctrines, Italy, on the other hand, clung to the powerful legacy of its past in virtue of which she proclaims the rights of the state, the preeminence of its authority, and the superiority of its ends. The very fact that the Italian political doctrine in the Middle Ages linked itself with the great political writers of antiquity, Plato and Aristotle, who in a different manner but with an equal firmness advocated a strong state and the subordination of individuals to it, is a sufficient index of the orientation of political philosophy in Italy. We all know how thorough and crushing the authority of Aristotle was in the Middle Ages. But for Aristotle the spiritual cement of the state is "virtue" not absolute virtue but political virtue, which is social devotion. His state is made up solely of its citizens, the citizens being either those who defend it with their arms or who govern it as magistrates. All others who provide it with the materials and services it needs are not citizens. They become such only in the corrupt forms of certain democracies. Society is therefore divided into two classes, the free men or citizens who give their time to noble and virtuous occupations and who profess their subjection to the state, and the laborers and slaves who work for the maintenance of the former. No man in this scheme is his own master. The slaves belong to the freemen, and the freemen belong to the state.

It was therefore natural that St. Thomas Aquinas the greatest political writer of the Middle Ages should emphasize the necessity of unity in the political field, the harm of plurality of rulers, the dangers and damaging effects of demagogy. The good of the state, says St. Thomas Aquinas, is unity. And who can procure unity more fittingly than he who is himself one? Moreover the government must follow, as far as possible, the course of nature and in nature power is always one. In the physical body only one organ is dominant—the heart; in the spirit only one faculty has sway—reason. Bees have one sole ruler; and the entire universe one sole sovereign—God. Experience shows that the countries, which are ruled by many, perish because of discord while those that are ruled over by one enjoy peace, justice, and plenty. The States which are not ruled by one are troubled by dissensions, and toil unceasingly. On the contrary the states which are ruled over by one king enjoy peace, thrive in justice and are gladdened by affluence.[2] The rule of the multitudes can not be sanctioned, for where the crowd rules it oppresses the rich as would a tyrant.[3]

Italy in the Middle Ages presented a curious phenomenon: while in practice the authority of the state was being dissolved into a multiplicity of competing sovereignties, the theory of state unity and authority was kept alive in the minds of thinkers by the memories of the Roman Imperial tradition. It was this memory that supported for centuries the fiction of the universal Roman Empire when in reality it existed no longer. Dante's *De Monarchia* deduced the theory of this empire conceived as the unity of a strong state. "Quod potest fieri per unum melius est per unum fieri quam plura," he says in the XIV chapter of the first book, and further on, considering the citizen as an instrument for the attainment of the ends of the state, he concludes that the individual must sacrifice himself for his country. "Si pars debet se exponere pro salute totius, cum homo siti pars quaedam civitatis ... homo pro patria debet exponere se ipsum." (lib. II. 8).

The Roman tradition, which was one of practice but not of theories—for Rome constructed the most solid state known to history with extraordinary statesmanship but with hardly any political writings—influenced considerably the founder of modern political science, Nicolo Machiavelli, who was himself in truth not a creator of doctrines but a keen observer of human nature who derived from the study of history practical maxims of political import. He freed the science of politics from the formalism of the scholastics and brought it close to concrete reality. His writings, an inexhaustible mine of practical remarks and precious observations, reveal dominant in him the state idea, no longer abstract but in the full historical concreteness of the national unity of Italy. Machiavelli therefore is not only the greatest of modern political writers, he is also the greatest of our countrymen in full possession of a national Italian consciousness. To liberate Italy, which was in his day "enslaved, torn and pillaged," and to make her more powerful, he would use any means, for to his mind the holiness of the end justified them completely. In this he was sharply rebuked by foreigners who were not as hostile to his means as they were fearful of the end which he propounded. He advocated therefore the constitution of a strong Italian state, supported by the sacrifices and by the blood of the citizens, not defended by mercenary troops; well-ordered internally, aggressive and bent on expansion. "Weak republics," he said, "have no determination and can never reach a decision." (Disc. I. c. 38). "Weak states were ever dubious in choosing their course, and slow deliberations are always harmful." (Disc. I. c. 10). And again: "Whoso undertakes to govern a multitude either in a régime of liberty or in a monarchy, without previously making sure of those who are hostile to the new order of things builds a short-lived state." (Disc. I. c. 16). And further on "the dictatorial authority helped and did not harm the Roman republic" (Disc. I. c. 34), and "Kings and republics lacking in national troops both for offense and defense should be ashamed of their existence." (Disc. I. c. 21). And again: "Money not only does not protect you but rather it exposes you to plundering assaults. Nor can there be a more false opinion than that which says that money is the sinews of war. Not money but good soldiers win battles." (Disc. I. II. c. 10). "The country must be defended with ignominy or with glory and in either way it is nobly defended." (Disc. III. c. 41). "And with dash and boldness people often capture what they never would have obtained by ordinary means." (Disc. III. c. 44). Machiavelli was not only a great political authority, he taught the mastery of energy and will. Fascism learns from him not only its doctrines but its action as well.

Different from Machiavelli's, in mental attitude, in cultural preparation, and in manner of presentation, G.B. Vico must yet be connected with the great Florentine from whom in a certain way he seems to proceed. In the heyday of "natural law" Vico is decidedly opposed to *ius naturale* and in his attacks against its advocates, Grotius, Seldenus and Pufendorf, he systematically assails the abstract, rationalistic, and utilitarian principles of the XVIII century. As Montemayor justly says:[4] "While the 'natural jurists', basing justice and state on utility and interest and grounding human certitude on reason, were striving to draft permanent codes and construct the perfect state, Vico strongly asserted the social nature of man, the ethical character of the juridical consciousness and its growth through the history of humanity rather than in sacred history. Vico therefore maintains that doctrines must begin with those subjects which take up and explain the entire course of civilization. Experience and not ratiocination, history and not reason must help human wisdom to understand the civil and political regimes which were the result not of reason or philosophy, but rather of common sense, or if you will of the social consciousness of man" and farther on (pages 373-374), "to Vico we owe the conception of history in its fullest sense as magistra vitae, the search after the humanity of history, the principle which makes the truth progress with time, the discovery of the political 'course' of nations. It is Vico who uttered the eulogy of the patrician 'heroic hearts' of the 'patres patriae' first founders of states, magnanimous defenders of the commonwealth and wise counsellors of politics. To Vico we owe the criticism of democracies, the affirmation of their brief existence, of their rapid disintegration at the hands of factions and demagogues, of their lapse first into anarchy, then into monarchy, when their degradation does not make them a prey of foreign oppressors. Vico conceived of civil liberty as subjection to law, as just subordination, of the private to the public interests, to the sway of the state. It was Vico who sketched modern society as a world of nations each one guarding its own imperium, fighting just and not inhuman wars. In Vico therefore we find the condemnation of pacifism, the assertion that right is actualized by bodily force, that without force, right is of no avail, and that therefore 'qui ab iniuriis se tueri non potest servus est.'"

It is not difficult to discern the analogies between these affirmations and the fundamental views and the spirit of Fascism. Nor should we marvel at this similarity. Fascism, a strictly Italian phenomenon, has its roots in the Risorgimento and the Risorgimento was influenced undoubtedly by Vico.

It would be inexact to affirm that the philosophy of Vico dominated the Risorgimento. Too many elements of German, French, and English civilizations had been added to our culture during the first half of the XIX century to make this possible, so much so that perhaps Vico might have remained unknown to the makers of Italian unity if another powerful mind from Southern Italy, Vincenzo Cuoco, had not taken it upon himself to expound the philosophy of Vico in those very days in which the intellectual preparation of the Risorgimento was being carried on.

An adequate account of Cuoco's doctrines would carry me too far. Montemayor, in the article quoted above, gives them considerable attention. He quotes among other things Cuoco's arraignment of Democracy: "Italy has fared badly at the hand of Democracy which has withered to their roots the three sacred plants of liberty, unity, and independence. If we wish to see these trees flourish again let us protect them in the future from Democracy."

The influence of Cuoco, an exile at Milan, exerted through his writings, his newspaper articles, and Vichian propaganda, on the Italian patriots is universally recognized. Among the regular readers of his *Giornale Italiano* we find Monti and Foscolo. Clippings of his articles were treasured by Mazzini and Manzoni, who often acted as his secretary, called him his "master in politics." [5]

The influence of the Italian tradition summed up and handed down by Cuoco was felt by Mazzini whose interpretation of the function of the citizen as duty and mission is to be connected with Vico's doctrine rather than with the philosophic and political doctrines of the French Revolution.

"Training for social duty," said Mazzini, "is essentially and logically unitarian. Life for it is but a duty, a mission. The norm and definition of such mission can only be found in a collective term superior to all the individuals of the country—in the people, in the nation. If there is a collective mission, a communion of duty ... it can only be represented in the national unity." [6] And farther on: "The declaration of rights, which all constitutions insist in copying slavishly from the French, express only those of the period ... which considered the individual as the end and pointed out only one half of the problem" and again, "assume the existence of one of those crises that threaten the life of the nation, and demand the active sacrifice of all its sons ... will you ask the citizens to face martyrdom in virtue of their rights? You have taught men that society was solely constituted to guarantee their rights and now you ask them to sacrifice one and all, to suffer and die for the safety of the 'nation?'"[7]

In Mazzini's conception of the citizen as instrument for the attainment of the nation's ends and therefore submissive to a higher mission, to the duty of supreme sacrifice, we see the anticipation of one of the fundamental points of the Fascist doctrine.

Unfortunately, the autonomy of the political thought of Italy, vigorously established in the works of Vico, nobly reclaimed by Vincenzo Cuoco, kept up during the struggles of the Risorgimento in spite of the many foreign influences of that period, seemed to exhaust itself immediately after the unification. Italian political thought which had been original in times of servitude, became enslaved in the days of freedom.

A powerful innovating movement, issuing from the war and of which Fascism is the purest expression, was to restore Italian thought in the sphere of political doctrine to its own traditions which are the traditions of Rome.

This task of intellectual liberation, now slowly being accomplished, is no less important than the political deliverance brought about by the Fascist Revolution. It is a great task which continues and integrates the Risorgimento; it is now bringing to an end, after the cessation of our political servitude, the intellectual dependence of Italy.

Thanks to it, Italy again speaks to the world and the world listens to Italy. It is a great task and a great deed and it demands great efforts. To carry it through, we must, each one of us, free ourselves of the dross of ideas and mental habits which two centuries of foreign intellectualistic tradition have heaped upon us; we must not only take on a new culture but create for ourselves a new soul. We must methodically and patiently contribute something towards the organic and complete elaboration of our doctrine, at the same time supporting it both at home and abroad with untiring devotion. We ask this effort of renovation and collaboration of all Fascists, as well as of all who feel themselves to be Italians. After the hour of sacrifice comes the hour of unyielding efforts. To our work, then, fellow countrymen, for the glory of Italy!

FOOTNOTES:

[1] Translated from the Italian.

[2] "civitates quae non reguntur ab uno dissenionibus laborant et absque pace fluctuant. E contrario civitates quae sub uno rege reguntur pace gaudent, iustitia florent et affluentia rerum laetantur." (De reg. princ. I. c. 2).

[3] "ideo manifustum est, quod multitudo est sicut tyrannuus, quare operationes multitudinis sunt iniustae. ergo non expedit multitudinem dominari." (Comm. In Polit. L. III. lectio VIII).

[4] Rivista internazionale di filosofia del diritto V. 351.

[5] Montemayor. Riv. Int. etc. p. 370.

[6] della unità italiana. Scritti, Vol. III.

[7] I sistemi e la democrazia. Scritti, Vol. VII.

THE PHILOSOPHIC BASIS OF FASCISM

ToC

by
GIOVANNI GENTILE

For the Italian nation the World War was the solution of a deep spiritual crisis. They willed and fought it long before they felt and evaluated it. But they willed, fought, felt and evaluated it in a certain spirit which Italy's generals and statesmen exploited, but which also worked on them, conditioning their policies and their action. The spirit in question was not altogether clear and self-consistent. That it lacked unanimity was particularly apparent just before and again just after the war when feelings were not subject to war discipline. It was as though the Italian character were crossed by two different currents which divided it into two irreconcilable sections. One need think only of the days of Italian neutrality and of the debates that raged between Interventionists and Neutralists. The ease with which the most inconsistent ideas were pressed into service by both parties showed that the issue was not between two opposing political opinions, two conflicting concepts of history, but actually between two different temperaments, two different souls.

For one kind of person the important point was to fight the war, either on the side of Germany or against Germany: but in either event to fight the war, without regard to specific advantages—to fight the war in order that at last the Italian nation, created rather by favoring conditions than by the will of its people to be a nation, might receive its test in blood, such a test as only war can bring by uniting all citizens in a single thought, a single passion, a single hope, emphasizing to each individual that all have something in common, something transcending private interests.

This was the very thing that frightened the other kind of person, the prudent man, the realist, who had a clear view of the mortal risks a young, inexperienced, badly prepared nation would be running in such a war, and who also saw—a most significant point—that, all things considered, a bargaining neutrality would surely win the country tangible rewards, as great as victorious participation itself.

The point at issue was just that: the Italian Neutralists stood for material advantages, advantages tangible, ponderable, palpable; the Interventionists stood for moral advantages, intangible, impalpable, imponderable—imponderable at least on the scales used by their antagonists. On the eve of the war these two Italian characters stood facing each other, scowling and irreconcilable—the one on the aggressive, asserting itself ever more forcefully through the various organs of public opinion; the other on the defensive, offering resistance through the Parliament which in those days still seemed to be the basic repository of State sovereignty. Civil conflict seemed inevitable in Italy, and civil war was in fact averted only because the King took advantage of one of his prerogatives and declared war against the Central Powers.

This act of the King was the first decisive step toward the solution of the crisis.

II

The crisis had ancient origins. Its roots sank deep into the inner spirit of the Italian people.

What were the creative forces of the *Risorgimento*? The "Italian people," to which some historians are now tending to attribute an important if not a decisive role in our struggle for national unity and independence, was hardly on the scene at all. The active agency was always an idea become a person—it was one or several determined wills which were fixed on determined goals. There can be no question that the birth of modern Italy was the work of the few. And it could not be otherwise. It is always the few who represent the self-consciousness and the will of an epoch and determine what its history shall be; for it is they who see the forces at their disposal and through those forces actuate the one truly active and productive force—their own will.

That will we find in the song of the poets and the ideas of the political writers, who know how to use a language harmonious with a universal sentiment or with a sentiment capable of becoming universal. In the case of Italy, in all our bards, philosophers and leaders, from Alfieri to Foscolo, from Leopardi to Manzoni, from Mazzini to Gioberti, we are able to pick up the threads of a new fabric, which is a new kind of thought, a new kind of soul, a new kind of Italy. This new Italy differed from the old Italy in something that was very simple but yet was of the greatest importance: this new Italy took life seriously, while the old one did not. People in every age had dreamed of an Italy and talked of an Italy. The notion of Italy had been sung in all kinds of music, propounded in all kinds of philosophy. But it was always an Italy that existed in the brain of some scholar whose learning was more or less divorced from reality. Now reality demands that convictions be taken seriously, that ideas become actions. Accordingly it was necessary that this Italy, which was an affair of brains only, become also an affair of hearts, become, that is, something serious, something alive. This, and no other, was the meaning of Mazzini's great slogan: "Thought and Action." It was the essence of the great revolution which he preached and which he accomplished by instilling his doctrine into the hearts of others. Not many others—a small minority! But they were numerous enough and powerful enough to raise the question where it could be answered—in Italian public opinion (taken in conjunction with the political situation prevailing in the rest of Europe). They were able to establish the doctrine that life is not a game, but a mission; that, therefore, the individual has a law and a purpose in obedience to which and in fulfillment of which he alone attains his true value; that, accordingly, he must make sacrifices, now of personal comfort, now of private interest, now of life itself.

No revolution ever possessed more markedly than did the Italian *Risorgimento* this characteristic of ideality, of thought preceding action. Our revolt was not concerned with the material needs of life, nor did it spring from elementary and widely diffused sentiments breaking out in popular uprisings and mass disturbances. The movements of 1847 and 1848 were demonstrations, as we would say today, of "intellectuals"; they were efforts toward a goal on the part of a minority of patriots who were standard bearers of an ideal and were driving governments and peoples toward its attainment. Idealism—understood as faith in the advent of an ideal reality, as a manner of conceiving life not as fixed within the limits of existing fact, but as incessant progress and transformation toward the level of a higher law which controls men with the very force of the idea—was the sum and substance of Mazzini's teaching; and it supplied the most conspicuous characteristic of our great Italian revolution. In this sense all the patriots who worked for the foundation of the new kingdom were Mazzinians—Gioberti, Cavour, Victor Emmanuel, Garibaldi. To be sure, our writers of the first rank, such as Manzoni and Rosmini, had no historical connection with Mazzini; but they had the same general tendency as Mazzini. Working along diverging lines, they all came together on the essential point: that true life is not the life which is, but also the life which ought to be. It was a conviction essentially religious in character, essentially anti-materialistic.

III

This religious and idealistic manner of looking at life, so characteristic of the *Risorgimento*, prevails even beyond the heroic age of the revolution and the establishment of the Kingdom. It survives down through Ricasoli, Lanza, Sella and Minghetti, down, that is, to the occupation of Rome and the systemization of our national finances. The parliamentary overturn of 1876, indeed, marks not the end, but rather an interruption, on the road that Italy had been following since the beginning of the century. The outlook then changed, and not by the capriciousness or weakness of men, but by a necessity of history which it would be idiotic in our day to deplore. At that time the fall of the Right, which had ruled continuously between 1861 and 1876, seemed to most people the real conquest of freedom.

To be sure the Right cannot be accused of too great scruple in respecting the liberties guaranteed by our Constitution; but the real truth was that the Right conceived liberty in a sense directly opposite to the notions of the Left. The Left moved from the individual to the State: the Right moved from the State to the individual. The men of the left thought of "the people" as merely the agglomerate of the citizens composing it. They therefore made the individual the center and the point of departure of all the rights and prerogatives which a régime of freedom was bound to respect.

The men of the Right, on the contrary, were firmly set in the notion that no freedom can be conceived except within the State, that freedom can have no important content apart from a solid régime of law indisputably sovereign over the activities and the interests of individuals. For the Right there could be no individual freedom not reconcilable with the authority of the State. In their eyes the general interest was always paramount over private interests. The law, therefore, should have absolute efficacy and embrace the whole life of the people.

This conception of the Right was evidently sound; but it involved great dangers when applied without regard to the motives which provoked it. Unless we are careful, too much law leads to stasis and therefore to the annihilation of the life which it is the State's function to regulate but which the State cannot suppress. The State may easily become a form indifferent to its content—something extraneous to the substance it would regulate. If the law comes upon the individual from without, if the individual is not absorbed in the life of the State, the individual feels the law and the State as limitations on his activity, as chains which will eventually strangle him unless he can break them down.

This was just the feeling of the men of '76. The country needed a breath of air. Its moral, economic, and social forces demanded the right to develop without interference from a law which took no account of them. This was the historical reason for the overturn of that year; and with the transference of power from Right to Left begins the period of growth and development in our nation: economic growth in industry, commerce, railroads, agriculture; intellectual growth in science, education. The nation had received its form from above. It had now to struggle to its new level, giving to a State which already had its constitution, its administrative and political organization, its army and its finance, a living content of forces springing from individual initiative prompted by interests which the *Risorgimento*, absorbed in its great ideals, had either neglected or altogether disregarded.

The accomplishment of this constitutes the credit side of the balance sheet of King Humbert I. It was the error of King Humbert's greatest minister, Francesco Crispi, not to have understood his age. Crispi strove vigorously to restore the authority and the prestige of the State as against an individualism gone rampant, to reassert religious ideals as against triumphant materialism. He fell, therefore, before the assaults of so-called democracy.

Crispi was wrong. That was not the moment for re-hoisting the time-honored banner of idealism. At that time there could be no talk of wars, of national dignity, of competition with the Great Powers; no talk of setting limits to personal liberties in the interests of the abstract entity called "State." The word "God," which Crispi sometimes used, was singularly out of place. It was a question rather of bringing the popular classes to prosperity, self-consciousness, participation in political life. Campaigns against illiteracy, all kinds of social legislation, the elimination of the clergy from the public schools, which must be secular and anti-clerical! During this period Freemasonry became solidly established in the bureaucracy, the army, the judiciary. The central power of the State was weakened and made subservient to the fleeting variations of popular will as reflected in a suffrage absolved from all control from above. The growth of big industry favored the rise of a socialism of Marxian stamp as a new kind of moral and political education for our proletariat. The conception of humanity was not indeed lost from view: but such moral restraints as were placed on the free individual were all based on the feeling that each man must instinctively seek his own well-being and defend it. This was the very conception which Mazzini had fought in socialism, though he rightly saw that it was not peculiar to socialism alone, but belonged to any political theory, whether liberal, democratic, or anti-socialistic, which urges men toward the exaction of rights rather than to the fulfillment of duties.

From 1876 till the Great War, accordingly, we had an Italy that was materialistic and anti-Mazzinian, though an Italy far superior to the Italy of and before Mazzini's time. All our culture, whether in the natural or the moral sciences, in letters or in the arts, was dominated by a crude positivism, which conceived of the reality in which we live as something given, something ready-made, and which therefore limits and conditions human activity quite apart from so-called arbitrary and illusory demands of morality. Everybody wanted "facts," "positive facts." Everybody laughed at "metaphysical dreams," at impalpable realities. The truth was there before the eyes of men. They had only to open their eyes to see it. The Beautiful itself could only be the mirror of the Truth present before us in Nature. Patriotism, like all the other virtues based on a religious attitude of mind, and which can be mentioned only when people have the courage to talk in earnest, became a rhetorical theme on which it was rather bad taste to touch.

This period, which anyone born during the last half of the past century can well remember, might be called the demo-socialistic phase of the modern Italian State. It was the period which elaborated the characteristically democratic attitude of mind on a basis of personal freedom, and which resulted in the establishment of socialism as the primary and controlling force in the State. It was a period of growth and of prosperity during which the moral forces developed during the *Risorgimento* were crowded into the background or off the stage.

IV

But toward the end of the Nineteenth Century and in the first years of the Twentieth a vigorous spirit of reaction began to manifest itself in the young men of Italy against the preceding generation's ideas in politics, literature, science and philosophy. It was as though they were weary of the prosaic bourgeois life which they had inherited from their fathers and were eager to return to the lofty moral enthusiasms of their grandfathers. Rosmini and Gioberti had been long forgotten. They were now exhumed, read, discussed. As for Mazzini, an edition of his writings was financed by the State itself. Vico, the great Vico, a formidable preacher of idealistic philosophy and a great anti-Cartesian and anti-rationalist, became the object of a new cult.

Positivism began forthwith to be attacked by neo-idealism. Materialistic approaches to the study of literature and art were refuted and discredited. Within the Church itself modernism came to rouse the Italian clergy to the need of a deeper and more modern culture. Even socialism was brought under the philosophical probe and criticized like other doctrines for its weaknesses and errors; and when, in France, George Sorel went beyond the fallacies of the materialistic theories of the Marxist social-democracy to his theory of syndicalism, our young Italian socialists turned to him. In Sorel's ideas they saw two things: first, the end of a hypocritical "collaborationism" which betrayed both proletariat and nation; and second, faith in a moral and ideal reality for which it was the individual's duty to sacrifice himself, and to defend which, even violence was justified. The anti-parliamentarian spirit and the moral spirit of syndicalism brought Italian socialists back within the Mazzinian orbit.

Of great importance, too, was nationalism, a new movement then just coming to the fore. Our Italian nationalism was less literary and more political in character than the similar movement in France, because with us it was attached to the old historic Right which had a long political tradition. The new nationalism differed from the old Right in the stress it laid on the idea of "nation"; but it was at one with the Right in regarding the State as the necessary premise to the individual rights and values. It was the special achievement of nationalism to rekindle faith in the nation in Italian hearts, to arouse the country against parliamentary socialism, and to lead an open attack on Freemasonry, before which the Italian bourgeoisie was terrifiedly prostrating itself. Syndicalists, nationalists, idealists succeeded, between them, in bringing the great majority of Italian youth back to the spirit of Mazzini.

Official, legal, parliamentary Italy, the Italy that was anti-Mazzinian and anti-idealistic, stood against all this, finding its leader in a man of unfailing political intuition, and master as well of the political mechanism of the country, a man sceptical of all high-sounding words, impatient of complicated concepts, ironical, cold, hard-headed, practical—what Mazzini would have called a "shrewd materialist." In the persons, indeed, of Mazzini and Giolitti, we may find a picture of the two aspects of pre-war Italy, of that irreconcilable duality which paralyzed the vitality of the country and which the Great War was to solve.

V

The effect of the war seemed at first to be quite in an opposite sense—to mark the beginning of a general *débâcle* of the Italian State and of the moral forces that must underlie any State. If entrance into the war had been a triumph of ideal Italy over materialistic Italy, the advent of peace seemed to give ample justification to the Neutralists who had represented the latter. After the Armistice our Allies turned their backs upon us. Our victory assumed all the aspects of a defeat. A defeatist psychology, as they say, took possession of the Italian people and expressed itself in hatred of the war, of those responsible for the war, even of our army which had won our war. An anarchical spirit of dissolution rose against all authority. The ganglia of our economic life seemed struck with mortal disease. Labor ran riot in strike after strike. The very bureaucracy seemed to align itself against the State. The measure of our spiritual dispersion was the return to power of Giolitti—the execrated Neutralist—who for five years had been held up as the exponent of an Italy which had died with the war.

But, curiously enough, it was under Giolitti that things suddenly changed in aspect, that against the Giolittian State a new State arose. Our soldiers, our genuine soldiers, men who had willed our war and fought it in full consciousness of what they were doing, had the good fortune to find as their leaders a man who could express in words things that were in all their hearts and who could make those words audible above the tumult.

Mussolini had left Italian socialism in 1915 in order to be a more faithful interpreter of "the Italian People" (the name he chose for his new paper). He was one of those who saw the necessity of our war, one of those mainly responsible for our entering the war. Already as a socialist he had fought Freemasonry; and, drawing his inspiration from Sorel's syndicalism, he had assailed the parliamentary corruption of Reformist Socialism with the idealistic postulates of revolution and violence. Then, later, on leaving the party and in defending the cause of intervention, he had come to oppose the illusory fancies of proletarian internationalism with an assertion of the infrangible integrity, not only moral but economic as well, of the national organism, affirming therefore the sanctity of country for the working classes as for other classes. Mussolini was a Mazzinian of that pure-blooded breed which Mazzini seemed somehow always to find in the province of Romagna. First by instinct, later by reflection, Mussolini had come to despise the futility of the socialists who kept preaching a revolution which they had neither the power nor the will to bring to pass even under the most favorable circumstances. More keenly than anyone else he had come to feel the necessity of a State which would be a State, of a law which would be respected as law, of an authority capable of exacting obedience but at the same time able to give indisputable evidence of its worthiness so to act. It seemed incredible to Mussolini that a country capable of fighting and winning such a war as Italy had fought and won should be thrown into disorder and held at the mercy of a handful of faithless politicians.

When Mussolini founded his Fasci in Milan in March, 1919, the movement toward dissolution and negation that featured the post-war period in Italy had virtually ceased. The Fasci made their appeal to Italians who, in spite of the disappointments of the peace, continued to believe in the war, and who, in order to validate the victory which was the proof of the war's value, were bent on recovering for Italy that control over her own destinies which could come only through a restoration of discipline and a reorganization of social and political forces. From the first, the Fascist Party was not one of believers but of action. What it needed was not a platform of principles, but an idea which would indicate a goal and a road by which the goal could be reached.

The four years between 1919 and 1923 inclusive were characterized by the development of the Fascist revolution through the action of "the squads." The Fascist "squads" were really the force of a State not yet born but on the way to being. In its first period, Fascist "squadrism" transgressed the law of the old régime because it was determined to suppress that régime as incompatible with the national State to which Fascism was aspiring. The March on Rome was not the beginning, it was the end of that phase of the revolution; because, with Mussolini's advent to power, Fascism entered the sphere of legality. After October 28, 1922, Fascism was no longer at war with the State; it *was* the State, looking about for the organization which would realize Fascism as a concept of State. Fascism already had control of all the instruments necessary for the upbuilding of a new State. The Italy of Giolitti had been superceded, at least so far as militant politics were concerned. Between Giolitti's Italy and the new Italy there flowed, as an imaginative orator once said in the Chamber, "a torrent of blood" that would prevent any return to the past. The century-old crisis had been solved. The war at last had begun to bear fruit for Italy.

VI

Now to understand the distinctive essence of Fascism, nothing is more instructive than a comparison of it with the point of view of Mazzini to which I have so often referred.

Mazzini did have a political conception, but his politic was a sort of integral politic, which cannot be so sharply distinguished from morals, religion, and ideas of life as a whole, as to be considered apart from these other fundamental interests of the human spirit. If one tries to separate what is purely political from his religious beliefs, his ethical consciousness and his metaphysical concepts, it becomes impossible to understand the vast influence which his credo and his propaganda exerted. Unless we assume the unity of the whole man, we arrive not at the clarification but at the destruction of those ideas of his which proved so powerful.

In the definition of Fascism, the first point to grasp is the comprehensive, or as Fascists say, the "totalitarian" scope of its doctrine, which concerns itself not only with political organization and political tendency, but with the whole will and thought and feeling of the nation.

There is a second and equally important point. Fascism is not a philosophy. Much less is it a religion. It is not even a political theory which may be stated in a series of formulae. The significance of Fascism is not to be grasped in the special theses which it from time to time assumes. When on occasion it has announced a program, a goal, a concept to be realized in action, Fascism has not hesitated to abandon them when in practice these were found to be inadequate or inconsistent with the principle of Fascism. Fascism has never been willing to compromise its future. Mussolini has boasted that he is a *tempista*, that his real pride is in "good timing." He makes decisions and acts on them at the precise moment when all the conditions and considerations which make them feasible and opportune are properly matured. This is a way of saying that Fascism returns to the most rigorous meaning of Mazzini's "Thought and Action," whereby the two terms are so perfectly coincident that no thought has value which is not already expressed in action. The real "views" of the *Duce* are those which he formulates and executes at one and the same time.

Is Fascism therefore "anti-intellectual," as has been so often charged? It is eminently anti-intellectual, eminently Mazzinian, that is, if by intellectualism we mean the divorce of thought from action, of knowledge from life, of brain from heart, of theory from practice. Fascism is hostile to all Utopian systems which are destined never to face the test of reality. It is hostile to all science and all philosophy which remain matters of mere fancy or intelligence. It is not that Fascism denies value to culture, to the higher intellectual pursuits by which thought is invigorated as a source of action. Fascist anti-intellectualism holds in scorn a product peculiarly typical of the educated classes in Italy: the *leterato*—the man who plays with knowledge and with thought without any sense of responsibility for the practical world. It is hostile not so much to culture as to bad culture, the culture which does not educate, which does not make men, but rather creates pedants and aesthetes, egotists in a word, men morally and politically indifferent. It has no use, for instance, for the man who is "above the conflict" when his country or its important interests are at stake.

By virtue of its repugnance for "intellectualism," Fascism prefers not to waste time constructing abstract theories about itself. But when we say that it is not a system or a doctrine we must not conclude that it is a blind praxis or a purely instinctive method. If by system or philosophy we mean a living thought, a principle of universal character daily revealing its inner fertility and significance, then Fascism is a perfect system, with a solidly established foundation and with a rigorous logic in its development; and all who feel the truth and the vitality of the principle work day by day for its development, now doing, now undoing, now going forward, now retracing their steps, according as the things they do prove to be in harmony with the principle or to deviate from it.

And we come finally to a third point.

The Fascist system is not a political system, but it has its center of gravity in politics. Fascism came into being to meet serious problems of politics in post-war Italy. And it presents itself as a political method. But in confronting and solving political problems it is carried by its very nature, that is to say by its method, to consider moral, religious, and philosophical questions and to unfold and demonstrate the comprehensive totalitarian character peculiar to it. It is only after we have grasped the political character of the Fascist principle that we are able adequately to appreciate the deeper concept of life which underlies that principle and from which the principle springs. The political doctrine of Fascism is not the whole of Fascism. It is rather its more prominent aspect and in general its most interesting one.

VII

The politic of Fascism revolves wholly about the concept of the national State; and accordingly it has points of contact with nationalist doctrines, along with distinctions from the latter which it is important to bear in mind.

Both Fascism and nationalism regard the State as the foundation of all rights and the source of all values in the individuals composing it. For the one as for the other the State is not a consequence—it is a principle. But in the case of nationalism, the relation which individualistic liberalism, and for that matter socialism also, assumed between individual and State is inverted. Since the State is a principle, the individual becomes a consequence—he is something which finds an antecedent in the State: the State limits him and determines his manner of existence, restricting his freedom, binding him to a piece of ground whereon he was born, whereon he must live and will die. In the case of Fascism, State and individual are one and the same things, or rather, they are inseparable terms of a necessary synthesis.

Nationalism, in fact, founds the State on the concept of nation, the nation being an entity which transcends the will and the life of the individual because it is conceived as objectively existing apart from the consciousness of individuals, existing even if the individual does nothing to bring it into being. For the nationalist, the nation exists not by virtue of the citizen's will, but as datum, a fact, of nature.

For Fascism, on the contrary, the State is a wholly spiritual creation. It is a national State, because, from the Fascist point of view, the nation itself is a creation of the mind and is not a material presupposition, is not a datum of nature. The nation, says the Fascist, is never really made; neither, therefore, can the State attain an absolute form, since it is merely the nation in the latter's concrete, political manifestation. For the Fascist, the State is always *in fieri*. It is in our hands, wholly; whence our very serious responsibility towards it.

But this State of the Fascists which is created by the consciousness and the will of the citizen, and is not a force descending on the citizen from above or from without, cannot have toward the mass of the population the relationship which was presumed by nationalism.

Nationalism identified State with Nation, and made of the nation an entity preëxisting, which needed not to be created but merely to be recognized or known. The nationalists, therefore, required a ruling class of an intellectual character, which was conscious of the nation and could understand, appreciate and exalt it. The authority of the State, furthermore, was not a product but a presupposition. It could not depend on the people—rather the people depended on the State and on the State's authority as the source of the life which they lived and apart from which they could not live. The nationalistic State was, therefore, an aristocratic State, enforcing itself upon the masses through the power conferred upon it by its origins.

The Fascist State, on the contrary, is a people's state, and, as such, the democratic State *par excellence*. The relationship between State and citizen (not this or that citizen, but all citizens) is accordingly so intimate that the State exists only as, and in so far as, the citizen causes it to exist. Its formation therefore is the formation of a consciousness of it in individuals, in the masses. Hence the need of the Party, and of all the instruments of propaganda and education which Fascism uses to make the thought and will of the *Duce* the thought and will of the masses. Hence the enormous task which Fascism sets itself in trying to bring the whole mass of the people, beginning with the little children, inside the fold of the Party.

On the popular character of the Fascist State likewise depends its greatest social and constitutional reform—the foundation of the Corporations of Syndicates. In this reform Fascism took over from syndicalism the notion of the moral and educational function of the syndicate. But the Corporations of Syndicates were necessary in order to reduce the syndicates to State discipline and make them an expression of the State's organism from within. The Corporation of Syndicates are a device through which the Fascist State goes looking for the individual in order to create itself through the individual's will. But the individual it seeks is not the abstract political individual whom the old liberalism took for granted. He is the only individual who can ever be found, the individual who exists as a specialized productive force, and who, by the fact of his specialization, is brought to unite with other individuals of his same category and comes to belong with them to the one great economic unit which is none other than the nation.

This great reform is already well under way. Toward it nationalism, syndicalism, and even liberalism itself, were already tending in the past. For even liberalism was beginning to criticize the older forms of political representation, seeking some system of organic representation which would correspond to the structural reality of the State.

The Fascist conception of liberty merits passing notice. The *Duce* of Fascism once chose to discuss the theme of "Force or consent?"; and he concluded that the two terms are inseparable, that the one implies the other and cannot exist apart from the other; that, in other words, the authority of the State and the freedom of the citizen constitute a continuous circle wherein authority presupposes liberty and liberty authority. For freedom can exist only within the State, and the State means authority. But the State is not an entity hovering in the air over the heads of its citizens. It is one with the personality of the citizen. Fascism, indeed, envisages the contrast not as between liberty and authority, but as between a true, a concrete liberty which exists, and an abstract, illusory liberty which cannot exist.

Liberalism broke the circle above referred to, setting the individual against the State and liberty against authority. What the liberal desired was liberty as against the State, a liberty which was a limitation of the State; though the liberal had to resign himself, as the lesser of the evils, to a State which was a limitation on liberty. The absurdities inherent in the liberal concept of freedom were apparent to liberals themselves early in the Nineteenth Century. It is no merit of Fascism to have again indicated them. Fascism has its own solution of the paradox of liberty and authority. The authority of the State is absolute. It does not compromise, it does not bargain, it does not surrender any portion of its field to other moral or religious principles which may interfere with the individual conscience. But on the other hand, the State becomes a reality only in the consciousness of its individuals. And the Fascist corporative State supplies a representative system more sincere and more in touch with realities than any other previously devised and is therefore freer than the old liberal State.

NATIONAL SOCIALISM

ToC

BASIC PRINCIPLES, THEIR APPLICATION
BY THE NAZI PARTY'S FOREIGN ORGANIZATION,
AND THE USE OF GERMANS ABROAD
FOR NAZI AIMS

Prepared in the Special Unit
Of the Division of European Affairs
by
RAYMOND E. MURPHY
FRANCIS B. STEVENS
HOWARD TRIVERS
JOSEPH M. ROLAND

ELEMENTS OF NAZI IDEOLOGY

The line of thought which we have traced from Herder to the immediate forerunners of the Nazi movement embodies an antidemocratic tradition which National Socialism has utilized, reduced to simple but relentless terms, and exploited in what is known as the National Socialist *Weltanschauung* for the greater aggrandizement of Nazi Germany. The complete agreement between the Nazi ideology and the previously described political concepts of the past is revealed in the forthcoming exposition of the main tenets of Naziism.

The Volk

Ernst Rudolf Huber, in his basic work *Verfassungsrecht des grossdeutschen Reiches (Constitutional Law of the Greater German Reich)* (document 1, *post* p. 155), published in 1939, states:

The new constitution of the German Reich ... is not a constitution in the formal sense such as was typical of the nineteenth century. The new Reich has no written constitutional declaration, but its constitution exists in the unwritten basic political order of the Reich. One recognizes it in the spiritual powers which fill our people, in the real authority in which our political life is grounded, and in the basic laws regarding the structure of the state which have been proclaimed so far. The advantage of such an unwritten constitution over the formal constitution is that the basic principles do not become rigid but remain in a constant, living movement. Not dead institutions but living principles determine the nature of the new constitutional order.[8]

In developing his thesis Huber points out that the National Socialist state rests on three basic concepts, the *Volk* or people, the Führer, and the movement or party. With reference to the first element, the *Volk*, he argues that the democracies develop their concept of the people from the wrong approach: They start with the concept of the state and its functions and consider the people as being made up of all the elements which fall within the borders or under the jurisdiction of the state. National Socialism, on the other hand, starts with the concept of the people, which forms a political unity, and builds the state upon this foundation.

There is no people without an objective unity, but there is also none without a common consciousness of unity. A people is determined by a number of different factors: by racial derivation and by the character of its land, by language and other forms of life, by religion and history, but also by the common consciousness of its solidarity and by its common will to unity. For the concrete concept of a people, as represented by the various peoples of the earth, it is of decisive significance which of these various factors they regard as determinants for the nature of the people. The new German Reich proceeds from the concept of the political people, determined by the natural characteristics and by the historical idea of a closed community. The political people is formed through the uniformity of its natural characteristics. Race is the natural basis of the people ... As a political people the natural community becomes conscious of its solidarity and strives to form itself, to develop itself, to defend itself, to realize itself. "Nationalism" is essentially this striving of a people which has become conscious of itself toward self-direction and self-realization, toward a deepening and renewing of its natural qualities.

This consciousness of self, springing from the consciousness of a historical idea, awakens in a people its will to historical formation: the will to action. The political people is no passive, sluggish mass, no mere object for the efforts of the state at government or protective welfare work ... The great misconception of the democracies is that they can see the active participation of the people only in the form of plebiscites according to the principle of majority. In a democracy the people does not act as a unit but as a complex of unrelated individuals who form themselves into parties ... The new Reich is based on the principle that real action of a self-determining people is only possible according to the principle of leadership and following.[9]

According to Huber, geographical considerations play a large part in the shaping of a people:

The people stands in a double relation, to its lands; it settles and develops the land, but the land also stamps and determines the people ... That a certain territory belongs to a certain people is not justified by state authority alone but it is also determined objectively by its historical, political position. Territory is not merely a field for the exercise of state control but it determines the nature of a people and thereby the historical purpose of the state's activity. England's island position, Italy's Mediterranean position, and Germany's central position between east and west are such historical conditions, which unchangeably form the character of the people. [10]

But the new Germany is based upon a "unity and entirety of the people"[11] which does not stop at geographical boundaries:

The German people forms a closed community which recognizes no national borders. It is evident that a people has not exhausted its possibilities simply in the formation of a national state but that it represents an independent community which reaches beyond such limits. [12]

The State justifies itself only so far as is helps the people to develop itself more fully. In the words of Hitler, quoted by Huber from *Mein Kampf*, "It is a basic principle, therefore, that the state represents not an end but a means. It is a condition for advanced human culture, but not the cause of it ... Its purpose is in the maintenance and advancement of a community of human beings with common physical and spiritual characteristics." [13]

Huber continues:

In the theory of the folk-Reich [*völkisches Reich*], people and state are conceived as an inseparable unity. The people is the prerequisite for the entire political order; the state does not form the people but the people moulds the state out of itself as the form in which it achieves historical permanence....[14]

The State is a function of the people, but it is not therefore a subordinate, secondary machine which can be used or laid aside at will. It is the form in which the people attains to historical reality. It is the bearer of the historical continuity of the people, which remains the same in the center of its being in spite of all changes, revolutions, and transformations. [15]

A similar interpretation of the role of the *Volk* is expounded by Gottfried Neesse in his *Die Nationalsozialistische Deutsche Arbeiterpartei—Versuch einer Rechtsdeutung*(*The National Socialist German Workers Party—An Attempt at Legal Interpretation*), published in 1935. From the National Socialist viewpoint, according to Neesse, the state is regarded not as an organism superior to the people but as an organization of the people: "In contrast to an organism, an organization has no inherent legality; it is dependent upon human will and has no definite mission of its own. It is a form in which a living mass shapes itself into unity, but it has no life of its own."[16] The people is the living organism which uses the organization of the state as the form in which it can best fulfil its mission. The law which is inherent in the people must be realized through the state.

But the central and basic concept of National Socialist political theory is the concept of the people:

In contrast to the state, the people form a true organism—a being which leads its own life and follows its own laws, which possesses powers peculiar to itself, and which develops its own nature independent of all state forms.... This living unity of the people has its cells in its individual members, and just as in every body there are certain cells to perform certain tasks, this is likewise the case in the body of the people. The individual is bound to his people not only physically but mentally and spiritually and he is influenced by these ties in all his manifestations.[17]

The elements which go to make up a people are beyond human comprehension, but the most important of them is a uniformity of blood, resulting in "a similarity of nature which manifests itself in a common language and a feeling of community and is further moulded by land and by history."[18] "The unity of the people is increased by its common destiny and its consciousness of a common mission."[19]

Liberalism gave rise to the concept of a "society-people" (*Gesellschaftsvolk*) which consisted of a sum of individuals, each of whom was supposed to have an inherent significance and to play his own independent part in the political life of the nation. National Socialism, on the other hand, has developed, the concept of the "community-people" (*Gemeinschaftsvolk*) which functions as a uniform whole.[20]

The people, however, is never politically active as a whole, but only through those who embody its will. The true will of a people can never be determined by a majority vote. It can only display itself in men and in movements, and history will decide whether these men or movements could rightly claim to be the representatives of the people's will.[21]

Every identification of the state with the people is false from a legal and untenable from a political standpoint ... The state is the law-forming organization and the law serves the inner order of the community; the people is the politically active organism and politics serve the outward maintenance of the community ... But law receives its character from the people and politics must reckon with the state as the first and most important factor.[22]

The "nation" is the product of this interplay and balance between the state and the people. The original and vital force of the people, through the organization of the state, realizes itself fully in the unified communal life of the nation:

The nation is the complete agreement between organism and organization, the perfect formation of a naturally grown being. ... *Nationalism* is nothing more than the outwardly directed striving to maintain this inner unity of people and state, and *socialism* is the inwardly directed striving for the same end.[23]

Dr. Herbert Scurla, Government Councilor and Reich's Minister for Science, Education, and Folk Culture, in a pamphlet entitled *Die Grundgedanken des Nationalsozialismus und das Ausland* (*Basic Principles of National Socialism With Special Reference to Foreign Countries*), also emphasizes the importance of the *Volk* in the National Socialist state. Dr. Scurla points out that National Socialism does not view the nation in the domocratic sense of a community to which the individual may voluntarily adhere.

The central field of force of the National Socialist consciousness is rather the folk, and this folk is in no case mere individual aggregation, i.e., collectivity as sum of the individuals, but as a unity with a peculiar two-sidedness, at the same time "essential totality" (M.H. Boehm). The folk is both a living creature and a spiritual configuration, in which the individuals are included through common racial conditioning, in blood and spirit. It is that force which works on the individual directly "from within or from the side like a common degree of temperature" (Kjellén) and which collects into the folk whatever according to blood and spirit belongs to it. This folk, point of departure and goal at the same time, is, in the National Socialist world-view, not only the field of force for political order, but as well the central factor of the entire world-picture. Neither individuals, as the epoch of enlightenment envisaged, nor states, as in the system of the dynastic and national state absolutism, nor classes, as conceived by Marxism, are the ultimate realities of the political order, but the peoples, who stand over against one another with the unqualifiable right to a separate existence as natural entities, each with its own essential nature and form.[24]

Dr. Scurla claims that National Socialism and Fascism are the strivings of the German and Italian people for final national unification along essentially different national lines natural to each of them. "What took place in Germany," he asserts, "was a political revolution of a total nature."[25] "Under revolution," he states, "we understand rather the penetration of the collective folk-mind [*gesamtvölkischen Bewusstseins*] into all regions of German life."[26] And, he concludes:

National Socialism is no invented system of rules for the political game, but the world-view of the German people, which experiences itself as a national and social community, and concedes neither to the state nor the class nor the individual any privileges which endanger the security of the community's right to live. [27]

Some of the most striking expressions of the race concept are found in *Die Erziehung im dritten Reich* (*Education in the Third Reich*), by Friedrich Alfred Beck, which was published in 1936. It is worthy of note that the tendency which may be observed in Huber (document I, *post* p. 155) and Neesse to associate the ideas of *Volk* and race is very marked with Beck. "All life, whether natural or spiritual, all historical progress, all state forms, and all cultivation by education are in the last analysis based upon the racial make-up of the people in question."[28] *Race* finds its expression in human life through the phenomenon of the *people*:

Race and *people* belong together. National Socialism has restored the concept of the people from its modern shallowness and sees in the people something different from and appreciably greater than a chance social community of men, a grouping of men who have the same external interests. By *people* we understand an entire living body which is racially uniform and which is held together by common history, common fate, a common mission, and common tasks. Through such an interpretation the people takes on a significance which is only attributed to it in times of great historical importance and which makes it the center, the content, and the goal of all human work. Only that race still possesses vital energy which can still bring its unity to expression in the totality of the people. The people is the space in which race can develop its strength. Race is the vital law of arrangement which gives the people its distinctive form. In the course of time the people undergoes historical transformations, but race prevents the loss of the people's own nature in the course of these transformations. Without the people the race has no life; without race the people has no permanence ... Education, from the standpoint of race and people, is the creation of a form of life in which the racial unity will be preserved through the totality of the people. [29]

Beck describes the politically spiritual National Socialist personality which National Socialist education seeks to develop, in the following terms:

Socialism is the direction of personal life through dependence on the community, consciousness of the community, feeling for the community, and action in the community; nationalism is the elevation of individual life to a unique (microcosmic) expression of the community in the unity of the personality. [30]

National Socialist education must stress the heroic life and teach German youth the importance of fulfilling their duty to the *Volk*.

Heroism is that force and that conviction which consecrates its whole life to the service of an idea, a faith, a task, or a duty even when it knows that the destruction of its own life is certain ... German life, according to the laws of its ideology, is heroic life ... All German life, every person belonging to the community of Germans must bear heroic character within himself. Heroic life fulfils itself in the daily work of the miner, the farmer, the clerk, the statesman, and the serving self-sacrifice of the mother. Wherever a life is devoted with an all-embracing faith and with its full powers to the service of some value, there is true heroism ... Education to the heroic life is education to the fulfilment of duty ... One must have experienced it repeatedly that the inner fruition of a work in one's own life has nothing to do with material or economic considerations, that man keeps all of his faculties alive through his obligation to his work and his devotion to his duty, and that he uses them in the service of an idea without any regard for practical considerations, before one recognizes the difference between this world of heroic self-sacrifice and the liberalistic world of barter. Because the younger generation has been brought up in this heroic spirit it is no longer understood by the representatives of the former era who judge the values of life according to material advantage ... German life is heroic life. Germany is not a mere community of existence and of interests whose only function is to insure the material and cultural needs of its members, but it also represents an elemental obligation on the part of the members. The eternal Germany cannot be drawn in on the map; it does not consist of the constitution or the laws of the state. This Germany is the community of those who are solemnly bound together and who experience and realize these eternal national values. This Germany is our eternal mission, our most sacred law ... The developing personality must be submerged in the living reality of the people and the nation from earliest youth on, must take an active and a suffering part in it. Furthermore the heroic life demands a recognition and experiencing of the highest value of life which man must serve with all his powers. This value can perhaps be recognized and presented theoretically in the schools but it can only be directly comprehended and personally experienced in the community of the people. Therefore all education must preserve this *direct connection with the community of the people* and school education must derive from it the form and substance of its instruction. [31]

This nationalism, which is based upon the laws of life, has nothing in common with the weak and presumptuous patriotism of the liberalistic world; it is not a gift or a favor, not a possession or a privilege, but it is the form of national life which we have won in hard battle and which suits our Nordic-German racial and spiritual heritage. In the nationalistic personality the powers and values which have been established in the socialistic personality will be purposefully exerted for the perfection of the temporal and eternal idea of life. [32]

The National Socialist idea of totality, therefore, and its manifestation in life of the national community form the principal substance of education in the Third Reich:

This idea of totality must be radically distinguished from the liberalistic conception of the mass. According to the liberalistic interpretation the whole consists of a summation of its parts. According to the National Socialist organic conception the whole comes before the parts; it does not arise from the parts but it is already contained in the parts themselves; all parts are microcosmic forms of the whole. This organic conception of the whole is the deepest natural justification of the basic political character of all organic life.[33]

Education, Beck continues, must present this total unity as it is manifested in the racial character of the people. Race is the most essential factor in the natural and spiritual unity of a people, and it is also the main factor which separates one people from another. The racial character of the people must determine the substance of education; this substance must be derived primarily from the life of the people.

Even in the specialized field of political science, Nazi education is concerned not with the structure of the state but with the role of the individual in the life of the people:

National Socialist political science concerns itself not with education to citizenship but with preparation for membership in the German people.... Not the structure of the state but the strength of a people determines the value and the strength of an individual life. The state must be an organization which corresponds to the laws of the people's life and assists in their realization. [34]

Such indeed is the supreme goal of all National Socialist education: to make each individual an expression of "the eternal German":

Whoever wishes fully to realize himself, whoever wishes to experience and embody the eternal German ideal within himself must lift his eyes from everyday life and must listen to the beat of his blood and his conscience ... He must be capable of that superhuman greatness which is ready to cast aside all temporal bonds in the battle for German eternity ... National Socialist education raises the eternal German character into the light of our consciousness ... National Socialism is the eternal law of our German life; the development of the eternal German is the transcendental task of National Socialist education.[35]

Racial Supremacy

The theory of the racial supremacy of the Nordic, i.e., the German, which was developed by Wagner and Stewart Chamberlain reaches its culmination in the writings of Alfred Rosenberg, the high priest of Nazi racial theory and herald of the *Herrenvolk* (master race). Rosenberg developed his ideas in the obscure phraseology of *Der Mythus des 20. Jahrhunderts (The Myth of the Twentieth Century)* (document 3, *post* p. 174). "The 'meaning of world history'," he wrote, "has radiated out from the north over the whole world, borne by a blue-eyed blond race which in several great waves determined the spiritual face of the world ... These wander-periods were the legendary migration of the Atlantides across north Africa, the migration of the Aryans into India and Persia; the migration of the Dorians, Macedonians, Latins; the migration of the Germanic tribes; the colonization of the world by the Germanic Occident."[36] He discusses at length Indian, Persian, Greek, Roman, and European cultures; in each case, he concludes, the culture is created by the ruling Nordic element and declines through the racial decay of the Nordics resulting from their intermixture with inferior races.

It has long been accepted, Rosenberg claims, that all the states of the west and their creative values have been generated by Germans; and it follows that if the Germanic blood were to vanish away completely in Europe all western culture would also fall to ruin.

Rosenberg acclaims the new faith of the blood which is to replace the non-German religion of Christianity. "A *new* faith is arising today: the myth of the blood, the faith to defend with the blood the divine essence of man. The faith, embodied in clearest knowledge, that the Nordic blood represents that *mysterium* which has replaced and overcome the old sacraments."[37]

Rosenberg accepts the classic German view of the *Volk*, which he relates closely to the concept of race. "The state is nowadays no longer an independent idol, before which everything must bow down; the state is not even an end but is only a means for the preservation of the folk ... Forms of the state change, and laws of the state pass away; the folk remains. From this alone follows that the nation is the first and *last*, that to which everything else has to be subordinated."[38] "The new thought puts folk and race higher than the state and its forms. It declares protection of the folk more important than protection of a religious denomination, a class, the monarchy, or the republic; it sees in treason against the folk a greater crime than high treason against the state."[39]

The essence of Rosenberg's racial ideas was incorporated in point 4 of the program of the Nazi Party, which reads as follows: "None but members of the nation [*Volk*] may be citizens of the State. None but those of German blood, whatever their creed, may be members of the nation. No Jew, therefore, may be a member of the nation."[40] After the Nazis came to power, this concept was made the basis of the German citizenship law of September 15, 1935.

Commenting upon point 4 of the Nazi program in his pamphlet, *Nature, Principles, and Aims of the NSDAP*, Rosenberg wrote:

An indispensable differentiation must be made sometime in the German *Volk* consciousness: The right of nationality should not represent something which is received in the cradle as a gift, but should be regarded as a good which must be earned. Although every German is a subject of the state, the rights of nationality should only be received when at the age of twenty or twenty-two he has completed his education or his military service or has finished the labor service which he owes to the state and after having given evidence of honorable conduct. The right to nationality, which must be earned, must become an opportunity for every German to strive for complete humanity and achievement in the service of the *Volk*. This consciousness, which must always be kept alive, will cause him to regard this earned good quite differently from the way it was regarded in the past and today more than ever.

The prevailing concept of state nationality completely ignores the idea of race. According to it whoever has a German passport is a German, whoever has Czech documents is a Czech, although he may have not a single drop of Czech blood in his veins ...

National Socialism also sees in the nature of the structure and leadership of the state an outflowing of a definite character in the *Volk*. If one permits a wholly foreign race subject to other impulses—to participate therein, the purity of the organic expression is falsified and the existence of the *Volk* is crippled....

This whole concept of the state [parliamentary democracy] is replaced by National Socialism with a basically different concept. National Socialism recognizes that, although the individual racial strains in German-speaking territory differ, they nevertheless belong to closely related races, and that many mixtures among the members of these different branches have produced new and vital strains, among them the complex but still *German* man, but that a mixture with the Jewish enemy race, which in its whole spiritual and physical structure is basically different and antagonistic and has strong resemblances to the peoples of the Near East, can only result in bastardization.[41]

True to the tradition of German imperialism, Rosenberg does not confine his ideas of racial supremacy to the Germans in the Reich alone. He even extends them to the United States, where he envisages the day when the awakening German element will realize its destiny in this country. In *Der Mythus des 20. Jahrhunderts*, for example, he writes, "After throwing off the worn-out idea upon which it was founded ... i.e., after the destruction of the idea represented by New York, the United States of North America has the great task ... of setting out with youthful energy to put into force the new racial-state idea which a few awakened Americans have already foreseen."[42]

This idea was developed at length by the German geopolitician, Colin Ross. In his book *Unser Amerika (Our America)* (document 4, *post* p. 178), published in 1936, Ross develops the thesis that the German element in the United States has contributed all that is best in American life and civilization and urges it to become conscious of its racial heritage and to prepare for the day when it may take over complete control of the country.

Reference was made in the preceding section to Beck's *Education in the Third Reich*. On the subject of racial supremacy Beck points out that certain new branches of learning have been introduced into the National Socialist schools and certain old ones have been given a new emphasis. The most important of these are the science of race and the cultivation of race (*Rassenkunde und Rassenpflege*), which teach the pupil to recognize and develop those racial powers which alone make possible the fullest self-realization in the national community. An awakening of a true racial consciousness in the people should lead to a "qualitative and quantitative" racial refinement of the German people by inducing a procreative process of selection which would reduce the strains of foreign blood in the national body. "German racial consciousness must have pride in the Nordic race as its first condition. It must be a feeling of the highest personal pride to belong to the Nordic race and to have the possibility and the obligation to work within the German community for the advancement of the Nordic race."[43] Beck points out that pupils must be made to realize "that the downfall of the Nordic race would mean the collapse of the national tradition, the disintegration of the living community and the destruction of the individual."[44]

Under the influence of war developments, which have given the Nazis a chance to apply their racial theories in occupied territories, their spokesmen have become increasingly open with regard to the political implications of the folk concept. In an article on "The Structure and Order of the Reich," published late in 1941, Ernst Rudolf Huber wrote, "this folk principle has found its full confirmation for the first time in the events of this war, in which the unity of the folk has been realized to an extent undreamed of through the return to the homeland of territories which had been torn from it and the resettlement of German folk-groups. Thus the awakening of Germandom to become a political folk has had a twofold result: the unity of the folk-community has risen superior to differences of birth or wealth, of class, rank, or denomination; and the unity of Germandom above all state boundaries has been consciously experienced in the European living-space [*Siedlungsraum*]."[45]

The Führer Principle

The second pillar of the Nazi state is the Führer, the infallible leader, to whom his followers owe absolute obedience. The Führer principle envisages government of the state by a hierarchy of leaders, each of whom owes unconditional allegiance to his immediate superior and at the same time is the absolute leader in his own particular sphere of jurisdiction.

One of the best expositions of the Nazi concept of the Führer principle is given by Huber in his *Constitutional Law of the Greater German Reich* (document 1, *post* p. 155):

The Führer-Reich of the [German] people is founded on the recognition that the true will of the people cannot be disclosed through parliamentary votes and plebiscites but that the will of the people in its pure and uncorrupted form can only be expressed through the Führer. Thus a distinction must be drawn between the supposed will of the people in a parliamentary democracy, which merely reflects the conflict of the various social interests, and the true will of the people in the Führer-state, in which the collective will of the real political unit is manifested ...

The Führer is the bearer of the people's will; he is independent of all groups, associations, and interests, but he is bound by laws which are inherent in the nature of his people. In this twofold condition: independence of all factional interests but unconditional dependence on the people, is reflected the true nature of the Führer principle. Thus the Führer has nothing in common with the functionary, the agent, or the exponent who exercises a mandate delegated to him and who is bound to the will of those who appoint him. The Führer is no "representative" of a particular group whose wishes he must carry out. He is no "organ" of the state in the sense of a mere executive agent. He is rather himself the bearer of the collective will of the people. In his will the will of the people is realized. He transforms the mere feelings of the people into a conscious will ... Thus it is possible for him, in the name of the true will of the people which he serves, to go against the subjective opinions and convictions of single individuals within the people if these are not in accord with the objective destiny of the people ... He shapes the collective will of the people within himself and he embodies the political unity and entirety of the people in opposition to individual interests ...

But the Führer, even as the bearer of the people's will, is not arbitrary and free of all responsibility. His will is not the subjective, individual will of a single man, but the collective national will is embodied within him in all its objective, historical greatness ... Such a collective will is not a fiction, as is the collective will of the democracies, but it is a political reality which finds its expression in the Führer. The people's collective will has its foundation in the political idea which is given to a people. It is present in the people, but the Führer raises it to consciousness and discloses it ...

In the Führer are manifested also the natural laws inherent in the people: It is he who makes them into a code governing all national activity. In disclosing these natural laws he sets up the great ends which are to be attained and draws up the plans for the utilization of all national powers in the achievement of the common goals. Through his planning and directing he gives the national life its true purpose and value. This directing and planning activity is especially manifested in the lawgiving power which lies in the Führer's hand. The great change in significance which the law has undergone is characterized therein that it no longer sets up the limits of social life, as in liberalistic times, but that it drafts the plans and the aims of the nation's actions ...

The Führer principle rests upon unlimited authority but not upon mere outward force. It has often been said, but it must constantly be repeated, that the Führer principle has nothing in common with arbitrary bureaucracy and represents no system of brutal force, but that it can only be maintained by mutual loyalty which must find its expression in a free relation. The Führer-order depends upon the responsibility of the following, just as it counts on the responsibility and loyalty of the Führer to his mission and to his following ... There is no greater responsibility than that upon which the Führer principle is grounded.[46]

The nature of the plebiscites which are held from time to time in a National Socialist state, Huber points out, cannot be understood from a democratic standpoint. Their purpose is not to give the people an opportunity to decide some issue but rather to express their unity behind a decision which the Führer, in his capacity as the bearer of the people's will, has already made:

That the will of the people is embodied in the Führer does not exclude the possibility that the Führer can summon all members of the people to a plebiscite on a certain question. In this "asking of the people" the Führer does not, of course, surrender his decisive power to the voters. The purpose of the plebiscite is not to let the people act in the Führer's place or to replace the Führer's decision with the result of the plebiscite. Its purpose is rather to give the whole people an opportunity to demonstrate and proclaim its support of an aim announced by the Führer. It is intended to solidify the unity and agreement between the objective people's will embodied in the Führer and the living, subjective conviction of the people as it exists in the individual members ... This approval of the Führer's decision is even more clear and effective if the plebiscite is concerned with an aim which has already been realized rather than with a mere intention. [47]

Huber states that the Reichstag elections in the Third Reich have the same character as the plebiscites. The list of delegates is made up by the Führer and its approval by the people represents an expression of renewed and continued faith in him. The Reichstag no longer has any governing or lawgiving powers but acts merely as a sounding board for the Führer:

It would be impossible for a law to be introduced and acted upon in the Reichstag which had not originated with the Führer or, at least, received his approval. The procedure is similar to that of the plebiscite: The lawgiving power does not rest in the Reichstag; it merely proclaims through its decision its agreement with the will of the Führer, who is the lawgiver of the German people. [48]

Huber also shows how the position of the Führer developed from the Nazi Party movement:

The office of the Führer developed out of the National Socialist movement. It was originally not a state office; this fact can never be disregarded if one is to understand the present legal and political position of the Führer. The office of the Führer first took root in the structure of the Reich when the Führer took over the powers of the Chancelor, and then when he assumed the position of the Chief of State. But his primary significance is always as leader of the movement; he has absorbed within himself the two highest offices of the political leadership of the Reich and has created thereby the new office of "Führer of the people and the Reich." That is not a superficial grouping together of various offices, functions, and powers ... It is not a union of offices but a unity of office. The Führer does not unite the old offices of Chancelor and President side by side within himself, but he fills a new, unified office. [49]

The Führer unites in himself all the sovereign authority of the Reich; all public authority in the state as well as in the movement is derived from the authority of the Führer. We must speak not of the state's authority but of the Führer's authority if we wish to designate the character of the political authority within the Reich correctly. The state does not hold political authority as an impersonal unit but receives it from the Führer as the executor of the national will. The authority of the Führer is complete and all-embracing; it unites in itself all the means of political direction; it extends into all fields of national life; it embraces the entire people, which is bound to the Führer in loyalty and obedience. The authority of the Führer is not limited by checks and controls, by special autonomous bodies or individual rights, but it is free and independent, all-inclusive and unlimited. It is not, however, self-seeking or arbitrary and its ties are within itself. It is derived from the people; that is, it is entrusted to the Führer by the people. It exists for the people and has its justification in the people; it is free of all outward ties because it is in its innermost nature firmly bound up with the fate, the welfare, the mission, and the honor of the people. [50]

Neesse, in his *The National Socialist German Workers Party—An Attempt at Legal Interpretation*, emphasizes the importance of complete control by the party leadership over all branches of the government. He says there must be no division of power in the Nazi state to interfere with the leader's freedom of action. Thus the Führer becomes the administrative head, the lawgiver, and the highest authority of justice in one person. This does not mean that he stands above the law. "The Führer may be outwardly independent, but inwardly he obeys the same laws as those he leads." [51]

The *leadership* (*Führung*) in the Nazi state is not to be compared with the *government* or *administration* in a democracy:

Führung is not, like government, the highest organ of the state, which has grown out of the order of the state, but it receives its legitimation, its call, and its mission from the people ... [52]

The people cannot as a rule announce its will by means of majority votes but only through its embodiment in one man, or in a few men. The principle of the *identity* of the ruler and those who are ruled, of the government and those who are governed has been very forcibly represented as the principle of democracy. But this identity ... becomes mechanistic and superficial if one seeks to establish it in the theory that the people are at once the governors and the governed ... A true organic identity is only possible when the great mass of the people recognizes its embodiment in one man and feels itself to be one nature with him ... Most of the people will never exercise their governing powers but only wish to be governed justly and well ... National Socialist *Führung* sees no value in trying to please a majority of the people, but its every action is dictated by service to the welfare of the people, even though a majority would not approve it. The mission of the *Führung* is received from the people, but the fulfilment of this mission and the exercise of power are free and must be free, for however surely and forcefully a healthy people may be able to make decisions in the larger issues of its destiny, its decisions in all smaller matters are confused and uncertain. For this reason, *Führung* must be free in the performance of its task ... The Führer does not stand for himself alone and can be understood not of himself, but only from the idea of a work to be accomplished ... Both the Führer and his following are subject to the idea which they serve; both are of the same substance, the same spirit, and the same blood. The despot knows only subjects whom he uses or, at best, for whom he cares. But the first consideration of the Führer is not his own advantage nor even, at bottom, the welfare of the people, but only service to the mission, the idea, and the purpose to which Führer and following alike are consecrated. [53]

The supreme position of Adolf Hitler as Führer of the Reich, which Huber and Neesse emphasize in the preceding quotations, is also stressed in the statements of high Nazi officials. For example, Dr. Frick, the German Minister of the Interior, in an article entitled "Germany as a Unitary State," which is included in a book called *Germany Speaks*, published in London in 1938, states:

The unity of the party and the state finds its highest realization in the person of the Leader and Chancelor who ... combines the offices of President and Chancelor. He is the leader of the National Socialist Party, the political head of the state and the supreme commander of the defense forces.[54]

It is interesting to note that, notwithstanding the generally recognized view as expressed in the preceding citations that the authority of the Führer is supreme, Hitler found it necessary in April 1942 to ask the Reichstag to confirm his power to be able at any time, if necessary, to urge any German to fulfil his obligations by all means which appear to the Führer appropriate in the interests of the successful prosecution of the war.[55] (The text of the resolution adopted by the Reichstag is included as document 5, *post* p. 183.)

Great emphasis is placed by the Nazi leaders on the infallibility of the Führer and the duty of obedience of the German people. In a speech on June 12, 1935, for instance, Robert Ley, director of the party organization, said, "Germany must obey like a well-trained soldier: the Führer, Adolf Hitler, is always right." Developing the same idea, Ley wrote in an article in the *Angriff* on April 9, 1942 (document 6, *post* p. 184): "Right is what serves my people; wrong is what damages it. I am born a German and have, therefore, only one holy mission: work for my people and take care of it." And with reference to the position of Hitler, Ley wrote:

The National Socialist Party is Hitler, and Hitler is the party. The National Socialists believe in Hitler, who embodies their will. Therefore our conscience is clearly and exactly defined. Only what Adolf Hitler, our Führer, commands, allows, or does not allow is our conscience. *We have no understanding for him who hides behind an anonymous conscience, behind God, whom everybody conceives according to his own wishes.*

These ideas of the Führer's infallibility and the duty of obedience are so fundamental in fact that they are incorporated as the first two commandments for party members. These are set forth in the *Organisationsbuch der NSDAP* (*Nazi Party Organization Book*) for 1940, page 7 (document 7, *post* p. 186). The first commandment is "The Führer is always right!" and the second is "Never go against discipline!"

In view of the importance attached to the Führer principle by the Nazis, it is only natural that youth should be intensively indoctrinated with this idea. Neesse points out that one of the most important tasks of the party is the formation of a "select group" or elite which will form the leaders of the future:

A party such as the NSDAP, which is responsible to history for the future of the German Reich, cannot content itself with the hope for future leaders but must create a strain of strong and true personalities which should offer the constantly renewed possibility of replacing leaders whenever it is necessary. [56]

Beck, in his work *Education in the Third Reich*, also insists that a respect for the Führer principle be inculcated in youth:

The educational value of the Hitler Youth is to be found in this community spirit which cannot be taught but can only be experienced ... But this cultivation of the community spirit through the experience of the community must, in order to avoid any conception of individual equality which is inconsistent with the German view of life, be based upon inward and outward recognition of the Führer principle ... In the Hitler Youth, the young German should learn by experience that there are no theoretical equal rights of the individual but only a natural and unconditional subordination to leadership. [57]

German writers often pretend that the Führer principle does not necessarily result in the establishment of a dictatorship but that it permits the embodiment of the will of the people in its leaders and the realization of the popular will much more efficiently than is possible in democratic states. Such an argument, for example, is presented by Dr. Paul Ritterbusch in *Demokratie und Diktatur* (*Democracy and Dictatorship*), published in 1939. Professor Ritterbusch claims that Communism leads to a dictatorial system but that the Nazi movement is much closer to the ideals of true democracy. The real nature of National Socialism, however, cannot be understood from the standpoint of the "pluralistic-party state." It does not represent a dictatorship of one party and a suppression of all others but rather an expression of the will and the character of the whole national community in and through one great party which has resolved all internal discords and oppositions within itself.

The Führer of this great movement is at once the leader and the expression of the national will. Freed from the enervating effects of internal strife, the movement under the guiding hand of the Führer can bring the whole of the national community to its fullest expression and highest development.

The highest authority, however, Hitler himself, has left no doubt as to the nature of Nazi Party leaders. In a speech delivered at the Sportpalast in Berlin on April 8, 1933, he said:

When our opponents say: "It is easy for you: you are a dictator"—We answer them, "No, gentlemen, you are wrong; there is no single dictator, but ten thousand, each in his own place." And even the highest authority in the hierarchy has itself only one wish, never to transgress against the supreme authority to which it, too, is responsible. We have in our movement developed this loyalty in following the leader, this blind obedience of which all the others know nothing and which gave to us the power to surmount everything.[58]

As has been indicated above, the Führer principle applies not only to the Führer of the Reich, Adolf Hitler, but to all the subordinate leaders of the party and the government apparatus. With respect to this aspect of the Führer principle, Huber (document 1, *post* p. 155), says:

The ranks of the public services are regarded as forces organized on the living principle of leadership and following: The authority of command exercised in the labor service, the military service, and the civil service is Führer-authority ... It has been said of the military and civil services that true leadership is not represented in their organization on the principles of command and obedience. In reality there can be no political leadership which does not have recourse to command and force as the means for the accomplishment of its ends. Command and force do not, of course, constitute the true nature of leadership, but as a means they are indispensable elements of every fully developed Führer-order.[59]

The Führer principle is officially recognized by the party, and the party interpretation thereof is set forth in the *Party Organization Book* (document 7 and charts 1 and 1-A, *post* pp. 186, 488, 489).

There are also included herein, as charts 2 and 2-A and 3 and 3-A (*post* pp. 490, 491, 492, 493), photostatic copies and translations of two charts from *Der nationalsozialistische Staat (The National Socialist State)* by Dr. Walther Gehl, published in 1935. These charts clearly show the concentration of authority in the Führer and the subordinate relation of the minor leaders in both the state and the party.

The Party: Leadership by an Elite Class
1. Functions of the Party

The third pillar of the Nazi state, the link between *Volk* and Führer, is the Nazi Party. According to Nazi ideology, all authority within the nation is derived ultimately from the people, but it is the party through which the people expresses itself. In *Rechtseinrichtungen und Rechtsaufgaben der Bewegung (Legal Organization and Legal Functions of the Movement)* (document 8, *post* p. 204), published in 1939, Otto Gauweiler states:

The will of the German people finds its expression in the party as the political organization of the people. It represents the political conception, the political conscience, and the political will. It is the expression and the organ of the people's creative will to life. It comprises a select part of the German people for "only the best Germans should be party members" ... The inner organization of the party must therefore bring the national life which is concentrated within itself to manifestation and development in all the fields of national endeavor in which the party is represented. [60]

Gauweiler defines the relationship of the party to the state in the following terms:

The party stands above and beside the state as the wielder of an authority derived from the people with its own sovereign powers and its own sphere of sovereignty ... The legal position of the party is therefore that of a completely sovereign authority whose legal supremacy and self-sufficiency rest upon the original independent political authority which the Führer and the movement have attained as a result of their historical achievements.[61]

Neesse states that "It will be the task of National Socialism to lead back the German people to an organic structure which proceeds from a recognition of the differences in the characters and possibilities of human beings without permitting this recognition to lead to a cleavage of the people into two camps."[62] This task is the responsibility of the party. Although it has become the only political party in Germany, the party does not desire to identify itself with the state. It does not wish to dominate the state or to serve it. It works beside it and cooperates with it. In this respect, Nazi Germany is distinguished from the other one-party states of Europe: "In the one-party state of Russia, the party rules over the state; in the one-party state of Italy, the party serves the state; but in the one-party state of Germany, the party neither serves the state nor rules over it directly but works and struggles together with it for the community of the people."[63] Neesse contends that the party derives its legal basis from the law inherent in the living organism of the German *Volk*:

The inner law of the NSDAP is none other than the inner law of the German people. The party arises from the people; it has formed an organization which crystallizes about itself the feelings of the people, which seemed buried, and the strength of the people, which seemed lost.[64]

Neesse states that the party has two great tasks—to insure the continuity of national leadership and to preserve the unity of the *Volk*:

The first main task of the party, which is in keeping with its organic nature, is to protect the National Socialist idea and to constantly renew it by drawing from the depths of the German soul, to keep it pure and clear, and to pass it on thus to coming generations: this is predominantly a matter of education of the people.

The second great task, which is in keeping with its organizational nature, is to form the people and the state into the unity of the nation and to create for the German national community forms which are ever new and suited to its vital development: this is predominantly a matter of state formation. These two tasks, one of which deals with substance and the other with function, belong together. It is as impossible to separate them as it is to split up the party into organism and organization, form and content.[65]

Huber (document 1, *post* p. 155) describes the tasks of the party in similar terms. He states that the party is charged with the "education of the people to a political people" through the awakening of the political consciousness of each individual; the inculcation of a "uniform political philosophy," that is, the teaching of Nazi principles; "the selection of leaders," including the choice and training of especially promising boys to be the Führers of the future; and the shaping of the "political will of the people" in accordance with the Führer's aims.[66]

The educational tasks of the party are stressed by Beck, who develops the idea that the *Volk* can be divided into three main groups, "a supporting, a leading, and a creative class."[67] It is the duty of the leading class, that is, the party, from which the creative class of leaders is drawn, to provide for the education of the supporting class.

Every member of the body of the people must belong to the politically supporting class, that is, each one who bears within himself the basic racial, spiritual, and mental values of the people ... Here no sort of leading or creative activity is demanded but only a recognition of the leading and creative will ... Only those are called to leadership in political life who have recognized the community-bound law of all human life in purest clarity and in the all-embracing extent of its validity and who will place all the powers of their personal lives with the help of a politically moral character in the service of the formation of community life ... From the politically leading class arise the politically creative personalities. These are the mysterious elemental forces which are beyond all explanation by human reason and which through their action and by means of the living idea within them give to the community of the people an expression which is fresh, young, and eternal. Here is the fulfilment of the highest and purest political humanity ... The education of the socialist personality is essentially the forming of the politically supporting class within the German people and the encouragement of those political tendencies which make a man a political leader. To educate to political creativeness is just as impossible as to educate to genius. Education can only furnish the spiritual atmosphere, can only prepare the spiritual living-space for the politically creative personality by forming a uniform political consciousness in the socialistic personality, and in the development of politically creative personalities it can at the most give special attention to those values of character and spirit which are of decisive importance for the development of this personality.[68]

Goebbels in *The Nature and Form of National Socialism* (document 2, *post* p. 170) emphasizes the responsibility of the party for the leadership of the state:

The party must always continue to represent the hierarchy of National Socialist leadership. This minority must always insist upon its prerogative to control the state. It must keep the way open for the German youth which wishes to take its place in this hierarchy. In reality the hierarchy has fewer rights than duties! It is responsible for the leadership of the state and it solemnly relieves the people of this responsibility. It has the duty to control the state in the best interests and to the general welfare of the nation.[69]

Dr. Frick, German Minister of the Interior, in his chapter in *Germany Speaks*, indicates the exclusive position of the party in the Third Reich:

National Socialist Germany, however, is not merely a unitary state: it is also a unitary nation and its governance is based on the principle of leadership ...

In National Socialist Germany, leadership is in the hands of an organized community, the National Socialist Party; and as the latter represents the will of the nation, the policy adopted by it in harmony with the vital interests of the nation is at the same time the policy adopted by the country ... The National Socialist Party is the only political party in Germany and therefore the true representative of the people...[70]

To Dr. Ley, the party is identical with the Führer. As he wrote in the *Angriff* on April 9, 1942 (document 6, *post* p. 184), "The National Socialist Party is Hitler, and Hitler is the party."

The role of the party in legislation, in political matters, and in the appointment of Government officials is indicated by the Führer's decree of May 29, 1941,[71] as amplified by the order of January 16, 1942, concerning its execution.[72] (Document 9, *post* p. 212). This order provides that all legislative proposals and proposed laws and decrees, as well as any proposed changes therein, must pass through and receive the approval of the Party Chancelry.

2. Party Membership

Details concerning the qualifications and duties of party members are contained in the *Party Organization Book* for 1940 (document 7, *post* p. 186).

Membership is finally confirmed by the issuance of a membership card or a membership book. Anyone who becomes a party member does not merely join an organization but he becomes a soldier in the German freedom movement and that means much more than just paying his dues and attending the members' meetings. He obligates himself to subordinate his own ego and to place everything he has in the service of the people's cause. Only he who is capable of doing this should become a party member. A selection must be made in accordance with this idea.

Readiness to fight, readiness to sacrifice, and strength of character are the requirements for a good National Socialist. Small blemishes, such as a false step which someone has made in his youth, should be overlooked; the contribution in the struggle for Germany should alone be decisive. The healthy will naturally prevail over the bad if the will to health finds sufficient support in leadership and achievement. Admission to the party should not be controlled by the old bourgeois point of view. The party must always represent the elite of the people. [73]

German blood is one of the prerequisites for party membership. The *Party Organization Book* for 1940 (document 7, *post* p. 186) also states, "Only those racial comrades who possess German citizenship are eligible for admission."[74]

Party members shall not exceed ten per cent of the German population of the region. "The ideal proportion of the number of party members to the number of racial comrades is set at ten per cent. This proportion is to apply also to the individual Province [Gau]."[75]

3. Pledges and Symbols of Allegiance

Party members take an oath of loyalty to the Führer in the following terms: "I pledge allegiance to my Führer, Adolf Hitler. I promise at all times to respect and obey him and the leaders whom he appoints over me."[76]

(a) The Hitler Salute

A pledge of allegiance to the Führer is also implied in the Nazi salute, which is usually accompanied by the greeting, "Heil Hitler." The phrase *mit deutschen Gruss*, which is commonly used as a closing salutation in letters, is another form of the Hitler greeting. *Knaurs Konversations-Lexikon* (*Knaur's Conversational Dictionary*), published in Berlin in 1934, contains the following definition:

German greeting, Hitler greeting: by raising the right arm; used by the old Germans with the spear as a greeting of arms [*Waffengruss*]. Communal greeting of the National Socialists; introduced into general use in 1933.

That this greeting was used by the Nazis as early as 1923 is demonstrated by a photograph which appeared in *Das Buch der NSDAP, Werden, Kampf and Ziel der NSDAP* (*The Book of the NSDAP, Growth, Struggle, and Goal of the NSDAP*) by Walter M. Espe (Berlin, 1934), illustration 34 (document 10, *post* p. 214).

In the same book (page 23 in the supplement entitled "*Die NSDAP*") the following distinction is made between the usual Nazi greeting and the Storm Troopers' salute:

While the German greeting consists merely in raising the right hand in any desired manner and represents rather a general comradely greeting, the SA salute is executed, in accordance with the specifications of the SA service regulations, by placing the left hand on the belt and raising the extended right arm.

The SA salute is to be given to all higher ranking leaders of the SA and the SS and of the veterans' organization which has been incorporated into the SA, as well as to the Army and the national and security police forces.

The comradely German greeting is to be exchanged between all equally ranking members of the SA and the SS and members of a corresponding rank in the Army, the police, the veterans' organization, the German air-sport league, the Hitler Youth, the railway guards, and the whole membership of the party so far as they are distinguishable by regulation uniforms.

(b) The Swastika

Early in its history the Nazi Party adopted the swastika banner as its official emblem.[77] It was designed by Hitler himself, who wrote in *Mein Kampf*:

I myself after countless attempts had laid down a final form: a flag with a background of red cloth, having a white circle, and, in its center, a black swastika....

As National Socialists we see our program in our flag. In the *red* we see the social idea of the movement, in the *white* the nationalistic idea, and in the *swastika* the fight for the victory of Aryan man and at the same time for the victory of the idea of creative work, which in itself always was and always will be anti-Semitic.[78]

The swastika banner came into general use after January 30, 1933 as a symbol of allegiance to the Hitler regime, but not until two years later was it made the German national flag by the Reich flag law of September 15, 1935.[79] Another law, decreed on April 7, 1937,[80] specified that:

The insignia which the NSDAP, its formations, and associated organizations use for their officers, their structure, their organization, and their symbols may not be used by other associations either alone or with embellishments.

It is interesting to note that party regulations forbid members to use passport photographs in which they appear in party uniform or wearing party insignia and that party members are forbidden to discuss foreign policy with foreigners unless they are officially designated by the Führer to do so. The pertinent regulations read:

Pass Photos on Identification Cards

Members of the NSDAP must not use pass photos which show the holder of any identification card in a uniform of the party or of any of its formations. It is also forbidden to use as pass photos pictures which show the person wearing a party button.

Conversations With Foreigners
It is forbidden to all party members to engage in discussions of foreign policy with foreigners. Only such persons as have been designated by the Führer are entitled to do so.[81]

The Totalitarian State

The Weimar Constitution, although never formally abrogated by the Nazis, was rendered totally ineffectual by two basic laws, promulgated within two months after the seizure of power by the party. The first of these was the "Decree of the Reich's President for the Protection of the People and State" (document 11-I, *post* p. 215), issued February 28, 1933, the day after the Reichstag was burned down. It suspended "until further notice"[82] articles of the Weimar Constitution guaranteeing essential democratic rights of the individual. Thus, according to article I of this decree, "restrictions on personal liberty, on the right of free expression of opinion, including freedom of the press, on the right of assembly and the right of association, and violations of the privacy of postal, telegraphic, and telephonic communications, and warrants for house-searches, orders for confiscations as well as restrictions on property, are also permissible beyond the legal limits otherwise prescribed."[83] The abrogation by the Nazis of these fundamental rights of democracy has never been repealed or amended. In fact, this decree represents the presupposition and confirmation of the police sway established throughout Germany by the Nazis.[84]

The second basic law, known as the "Enabling Act," the "Law To Remove the Distress of People and State," of March 24, 1933 (document 11-II, *post* p. 217), swept away parliamentary government entirely. By abrogating the pertinent articles of the Weimar Constitution, it enabled the Nazi Cabinet under Hitler's chancelorship to appropriate money and legislate without any responsibility to the Reichstag or any obligation to respect the Constitution.

The dissolution of democracy in Germany was sealed by the unification of the authoritarian Nazi Party with the German state. Soon after the party came to power in 1933, steps were taken to effect and secure this unity. The process is described by Huber (document 1, *post* p. 155) as follows:

On July 14, 1933 was issued the law against the formation of new parties which raised the NSDAP to the only political party in Germany [document 11-III] ... The overthrow of the old party-state was accompanied by the construction of the new movement-state [*Bewegungsstaat*]. Out of a political fighting organization the NSDAP grew to a community capable of carrying the state and the nation. This process was accomplished step by step in the first months after the National Socialist seizure of power. The assumption of the office of Chancelor by the Führer of the movement formed the basis for this development. Various party leaders were appointed as *Reichsminister*; the governors of the provinces were national leaders or *Gauleiter* of the party, such as General von Epp; the Prussian government officials are as a rule *Gauleiter* of the party; the Prussian police chiefs are mostly high-ranking SA leaders. By this system of a union of the personnel of the party and state offices the unity of party and state was achieved.[85]

The culmination of this development was reached in the "Law To Safeguard the Unity of Party and State," of December 1, 1933 (document 11-IV, *post* p. 221), which proclaimed the NSDAP "the bearer of the German state-idea and indissolubly joined to the state." In order to guarantee the complete cooperation of the party and SA with the public officials, the Führer's Deputy and the Chief of Staff of the SA were made members of the Cabinet.

With regard to the relation between the party and the state, Neesse writes:

The NSDAP is not a structure which stands under direct state control, to which single tasks of public administration are entrusted by the state, but it holds and maintains is claim to totality as the "bearer of the German state-idea" in all fields relating to the community—regardless of how various single functions are divided between the organization of the party and the organization of the state.[86]

To maintain cooperation between the party and state organizations, the highest state offices are given to the men holding the corresponding party offices. Gauweiler (document 8, *post* p. 204) attributes to the party supreme leadership in all phases of national life. Thus the state becomes merely an administrative machine which the party has set up in accordance with and for the accomplishment of its aims:

As the responsible bearer and shaper of the destiny of the whole German nation the party has created an entirely new state, for that which sought to foist itself upon her as a state was simply the product of a deep human confusion. The state of the past and its political ideal had never satisfied the longing of the German people. The National Socialist movement already carried its state within itself at the time of its early struggles. It was able to place the completely formed body of its own state at the disposal of the state which it had taken over.[87]

The official party interpretation of the relation between party and state, as set forth in the *Party Organization Book* for 1940, appears in the Appendix as document 7 (*post* p. 186).

Goebbels in his lecture on *The Nature and Form of National Socialism* (document 2, *post* p. 170) stressed the importance of *Gleichschaltung* or the penetration of Nazi ideology into all fields of national life. This to his mind must be the result of the National Socialist revolution. The same aims, ideals, and standards must be applied to economics and to politics, to cultural and social development, to education and religion, and to foreign and domestic relations.

The result of this concept of the totalitarian state has been the compulsory regimentation of all phases of German life to conform to the pattern established by the party. The totalitarian state does not recognize personal liberties for the individual. The legal position of the individual citizen in the Third Reich is clearly set forth by Huber (document 1, *post* p. 155):

Not until the nationalistic political philosophy had become dominant could the liberalistic idea of basic rights be really overcome. The concept of personal liberties of the individual as opposed to the authority of the state had to disappear; it is not to be reconciled with the principle of the nationalistic Reich. There are no personal liberties of the individual which fall outside of the realm of the state and which must be respected by the state. The member of the people, organically connected with the whole community, has replaced the isolated individual; he is included in the totality of the political people and is drawn into the collective action. There can no longer be any question of a private sphere, free of state influence, which is sacred and untouchable before the political unity. The constitution of the nationalistic Reich is therefore not based upon a system of inborn and inalienable rights of the individual.[88]

In place of these rights the constitution of the Third Reich guarantees to the individual his place in the community of the people:

The legal position of the individual member of the people forms an entirely new concept which is indispensable for the construction of a nationalistic order. The legal position of the individual is always related to the community and conditioned by duty. It is developed not for the sake of the individual but for the community, which can only be filled with life, power, and purpose when a suitable field of action is insured for the individual member. Without a concrete determination of the individual's legal position there can be no real community.

This legal position represents the organic fixation of the individual in the living order. Rights and obligations arise from the application of this legal position to specific individual relationships ... But all rights must be regarded as duty-bound rights. Their exercise is always dependent upon the fulfilment by the individual of those duties to which all rights are subordinate ...[89]

The concept of private property in the totalitarian state is also at variance with the democratic concept of private property. In the Third Reich the holder of property is considered merely as a manager responsible to the *Volk* for the use of the property in the common interest. Huber sets forth the Nazi view in the following words:

"Private property" as conceived under the liberalistic economic order was a reversal of the true concept of property. This "private property" represented the right of the individual to manage and to speculate with inherited or acquired property as he pleased, without regard for the general interests ... German socialism had to overcome this "private," that is, unrestrained and irresponsible view of property. All property is common property. The owner is bound by the people and the Reich to the responsible management of his goods. His legal position is only justified when he satisfies this responsibility to the community.[90]

Pursuant to this view of the nature of ownership, property may be confiscated whenever the state decides that public management would be in the interests of the community, or if the owner is found guilty of irresponsible management, in which case no compensation is paid him.

Reference has been made to the appointment of party members to important state offices. Gauweiler (document 8, *post* p. 204) points out that the party insured the infusion of the entire structure of the state with its ideology through the civil-service law (*Beamtengesetz*) of January 26, 1937,[91] which provides that a person appointed to a civil-service position must be "filled with National Socialist views, since only thus can he be an executor of the will of the state which is carried by the NSDAP. It demands of him that he be ready at all times to exert himself unreservedly in behalf of the National Socialist state and that he be aware of the fact that the NSDAP, as the mouthpiece of the people's will, is the vital force behind the concept of the German state."[92]

The infiltration of party members into the civil service has now proceeded to such a point that early in 1942 Pfundtner, the Secretary of State in the German Ministry of the Interior, could write in the periodical *Akademie für deutsches Recht*:

The German civil servant must furthermore be a National Socialist to the marrow of his bones and must be a member of the party or of one of its formations. The state will primarily see to it that the Young Guard of the movement is directed toward a civil-service career and also that the civil servant takes an active part in the party so that the political idea and service of the state become closely welded.[93]

FOOTNOTES TO FIRST SECTION

[8] Huber, *Verfassungsrecht des grossdeutschen Reiches* (Hamburg, 1939), pp. 54-55.
[9] *Ibid.*, pp. 153-155.
[10] *Ibid.*, pp. 156-157.
[11] *Ibid.*, p. 157.
[12] *Ibid.*, p. 158.
[13] *Ibid.*, p. 163.
[14] *Ibid.*, p. 164.
[15] *Ibid.*, pp. 165-166.
[16] Neesse, *Die Nationalsozialistische Deutsche Arbeiterpartei—Versuch einer Rechtsdeutung* (Stuttgart, 1935), p. 44.
[17] *Ibid.*, p. 51.
[18] *Ibid.*, p. 54.
[19] *Ibid.*, p. 58.
[20] *Ibid.*, pp. 54-56.
[21] *Ibid.*, p. 59.
[22] *Ibid.*, pp. 60-61.
[23] *Ibid.*, pp. 65-66.
[24] Scurla, *Die Grundgedanken des Nationalsozialismus und das Ausland* (Berlin, 1938), pp. 10-11.
[25] *Ibid.*, p. 9.
[26] *Ibid.*
[27] *Ibid.*, p. 13.

[28] Beck, *Die Erziehung im dritten Reich* (Dortmund and Breslau, 1936), p. 20.
[29] *Ibid.*, pp. 20-21.
[30] *Ibid.*, p. 35.
[31] *Ibid.*, pp. 52-55.
[32] *Ibid.*, p. 46.
[33] *Ibid.*, p. 57.
[34] *Ibid.*, p. 118.
[35] *Ibid.*, p. 140.
[36] Rosenberg, *Der Mythus des 20. Jahrhunderts* (Munich, 1935), p. 28 (1st ed. 1930).
[37] *Ibid.*, p. 114.
[38] *Ibid.*, p. 479.
[39] *Ibid.*, p. 542.
[40] Gottfried Feder, *The Programme of the Party of Hitler* (translated by E.T.S. Dugdale: Munich, 1932), p. 18.
[41] Rosenberg, *Wesen, Grundsätze und Ziele der NSDAP* (Munich, 1933), pp. 16-18 (1st ed. 1922).
[42] Rosenberg, *Der Mythus des 20. Jahrhunderts*, p. 673.
[43] Beck, *op. cit.*, p. 110.
[44] *Ibid.*, p. 110.
[45] Huber, "*Aufbau und Gefüge des Reiches*," published in the book *Idee und Ordnung des Reiches* (ed. by Huber: Hamburg, Hanseatische Verlagsanstalt, 1941), p. 12.
[46] Huber, *Verfassungsrecht des grossdeutschen Reiches* (Hamburg, 1939), pp. 194-198.
[47] *Ibid.*, pp. 199-200.
[48] *Ibid.*, pp. 207-208.
[49] *Ibid.*, pp. 213-214.
[50] *Ibid.*, p. 230.
[51] Neesse, *op. cit.*, p. 146.
[52] *Ibid.*, p. 143.
[53] *Ibid.*, pp. 144-147.
[54] *Germany Speaks* (containing articles by twenty-one leading members of the Nazi Party and the German Government: London, 1938), p. 31.
[55] *Reichsgesetzblatt* (1942), p. 247. (All citations to the *Reichsgesetzblatt* refer to part I thereof.)
[56] Neesse, *op. cit.*, p. 150.
[57] Beck, *op. cit.*, p. 131.
[58] *My New Order*, p. 159.
[59] Huber, *Verfassungsrecht des grossdeutschen Reiches* (Hamburg, 1939), p. 410.
[60] Gauweiler, *Rechtseinrichtungen und Rechtsaufgaben der Bewegung* (Munich, 1939), p. 2.
[61] *Ibid.*, p. 9.
[62] Neesse, *op. cit.*, p. 71.
[63] *Ibid.*, p. 119.
[64] *Ibid.*, p. 126.
[65] *Ibid.*, pp. 139-140.
[66] Huber, *Verfassungsrecht des grossdeutschen Reiches* (Hamburg, 1939), pp. 293-296.
[67] Beck, *op. cit.*, p. 37.
[68] *Ibid.*, pp. 37-38.
[69] Goebbels, *op. cit.*, p. 19.
[70] *Germany Speaks*, pp. 30-31.
[71] *Reichsgesetzblatt* (1941), p. 295.
[72] *Ibid.*, (1942), p. 35.
[73] *Organisationsbuch der NSDAP* (ed. by the National Organizational Director of the NSDAP: Munich, 1940), p. 5.
[74] *Ibid.*, p. 6b.
[75] *Ibid.*, p. 6d.
[76] *Ibid.*

[77] The German pocket reference book for current events (*Taschen-Brockhaus zum Zeitgeschehen*: Leipzig, 1942) states that the swastika banner was designed by Hitler for the NSDAP in 1919.

[78] Adolf Hitler, *Mein Kampf* (Munich, Verlag Frank Eher, G.m.b.H., 1933 [copyright 1925]), pp. 556-557.

[79] *Reichsgesetzblatt* (1935), p. 1145.

[80] *Ibid.* (1937), p. 442.

[81] *Organisationsbuch der NSDAP* (Munich, 1940), p. 8.

[82] *Reichsgesetzblatt* (1933), p. 83.

[83] *Ibid.*

[84] In his book *Die deutsche Polizei* (*The German Police*) (Darmstadt, L.C. Wittich Verlag, 1941), p. 24, the prominent Nazi police official, Dr. Werner Best, wrote that this law "is to be regarded not as a 'police law'—that is, as the regulation of police functions and activities—but as the expression of the new conception of the state as it has been transformed by the National Socialist revolution, from which the new 'police' concept is derived." Also, this law was for the police "the confirmation that the work already begun was in agreement with the law giving will of the Supreme Leadership of the Reich."

[85] Huber, *Verfassungsrecht des grossdeutschen Reiches* (Hamburg, 1939) p. 288.

[86] Neesse, *op. cit.*, p. 131.

[87] Gauweiler, *op. cit.*, p. 3.

[88] Huber, *Verfassungsrecht des grossdeutschen Reiches* (Hamburg, 1939), p. 361.

[89] *Ibid.*, pp. 365-366.

[90] *Ibid.*, pp. 372-373.

[91] *Reichsgesetzblatt* (1937), pp. 39-70.

[92] Gauweiler, *op. cit.*, p. 156.

[93] Reported in a bulletin of the official German news agency, DNB, Apr. 14, 1942.

NAZI AIMS AND METHODS
Political Aims

The political aims of National Socialism have been written so clearly in history in the past 10 years that it does not appear necessary to discuss them at length here.

The detailed program of the Nazi Party consists of the 25 points which were adopted on February 24, 1920 at a party mass meeting in Munich. (The 25-point program appears in the Appendix as document 12, *post* p. 222.) The points of particular interest in this study are the first four, which are set forth below:

1. We demand the union of all Germans to form a Great Germany on the basis of the right of the self-determination enjoyed by nations.

2. We demand equality of rights for the German People in its dealings with other nations, and abolition of the Peace Treaties of Versailles and St. Germain.

3. We demand land and territory (colonies) for the nourishment of our people and for settling our superfluous population.

4. None but members of the nation may be citizens of the State. None but those of German blood, whatever their creed, may be members of the nation. No Jew, therefore, may be a member of the nation.[94]

1. Internal Objectives

A statement of the internal objectives of National Socialism is made by Gauweiler in his *Legal Organization and Legal Functions of the Movement* (document 8, *post* p. 204). The laws of the Reich must seek to establish and promote the five basic values recognized by Nazi ideology:

1. Race: The legal protection of the race, which has created a new concept of nationality [*Volkszugehörigkeit*], is consciously put in first place, for the most significant historical principle which has been established by the victory of National Socialism is that of the necessity for keeping race and blood pure. All human mistakes and errors can be corrected except one: "the error regarding the importance of maintaining the basic values of a nation."

The purpose of this legal protection of the basic value of *race* must be the prevention for all time of a further mixture of German blood with foreign blood, as well as the prevention of continued procreation of racially unworthy and undesirable members of the people.

2. Soil [*Boden*]: The living-space and the basis for the food supply of the German people are its territory and soil. The farmer is the first and deepest representative of the people since he nourishes the people from the fertility of the earth and he maintains the nation through the fertility of his own family. Here National Socialism had to accomplish two great legal ends: the reestablishment and the protection of the farmer class and the securing of its land for the farmer family.

3. Work: The nation's work as a basic national value is grounded on the leading concept of "work of the hands and of the head" within and for the community of the people and the elevation of work to the only criterion for the value of an individual within the community. In place of the idea of class warfare, National Socialism had to establish the national community legally; in place of the defamation of work and its degradation to an object of barter, National Socialism had to raise it to an ethical duty and the right to work had to become the most clearly defined personal right of the individual. The concept of the honor of work had to be established as the basic concept of the national honor.

4. The Reich: With the securing of the three basic values of race, soil, and work arises the National Socialist Reich.

The infusion of foreign cultural and legal influences in Germany was a consequence of the weakening of the central authority of the German Reich since the Middle Ages. The creation and insuring of a strong central authority in contrast to the disorganized, federalistic system of the Weimar Republic became one of the principal lines of National Socialist legal policy. In consequence of the National Socialist revolution, the Reich took on the legal form of a totalitarian state and received a supreme and completely authoritative lawgiver in the person of the Führer. The principle of a division of power could no longer maintain itself: The formulation, the interpretation, and the execution of the law are all performed by the Führer himself or under his authority.

5. Honor: The fifth great value of the nation is its honor. The honor of the people, the Reich, the party, the Führer, and the individual citizen are all regarded as goods to be protected by law. The basis of national honor is loyalty. National Socialist criminal law is therefore essentially organized as a system of punishment for breaches of faith. Every crime and offense against the community is a breach of faith which must result in loss of honor.[95]

2. Foreign Policy

The close connection between the internal political program of the National Socialist movement, as expressed in the foregoing paragraphs, and its foreign policy was indicated by Hitler when he wrote in *Mein Kampf* (document 13-I, *post* p. 226):

As National Socialists we can further set forth the following principle with regard to the nature of the foreign policy of a folk-state:

It is the task of the foreign policy of a folk-state to secure the existence on this planet of the race which is encompassed by the state and at the same time to establish a healthy, viable, natural relation between the number and growth of the folk on the one hand and the size and quality of its soil and territory on the other hand.[96]

And in the same work he states:

Yes, we can only learn from the past that we must undertake the setting of aims for our political activity in two directions:*Soil and territory as the goal of our foreign policy, and a new, philosophically firm and uniform foundation as the goal of our domestic political activity.*[97]

The political objectives of National Socialism, then, by definition of Hitler himself, are the internal unification of the German people and external expansion.

While the Nazis have never concealed the first of these objectives, the second was the subject for a great deal of dissimulation up to the outbreak of the present war. Typical of the false front which the Nazis presented to the outside world with reference to their foreign policy objectives are the statements made by Dr. Scurla in *Basic Principles of National Socialism With Special Reference to Foreign Countries*. Dr. Scurla quotes Hitler's speech of May 17, 1933 in which he said, "We see the European nations around us as given facts. French, Poles, etc., are our neighbor peoples, and we know that no conceivable historic occurrence could change this reality,"[98] and comments:

This folk principle, which has grown out of the National Socialist ideology, implies the recognition of the independence and the equal rights of each people. We do not see how anyone can discern in this a "pan-Germanic" and imperialistic threat against our neighbors. This principle does not admit the difference between "great powers" and "minor states," between majority peoples and minorities. It means at the same time a clear rejection of any imperialism which aims at the subjugation of foreign peoples or the denationalization of alien populations. It demands the unqualified acknowledgment of the right to live of every folk, and of every folk-group, which is forced to live as a foreign group in another state. The western European national state together with its parliamentary democracy was not able to do justice to the natural and living entities, the peoples, in their struggle for existence.[99]

Farther on in the same work Scurla states:

Out of its fundamental ideologic view, however, Germany rejects every form of imperialism, even that of peaceful penetration. It is unable to concede to any people the authority to develop ideas and ways of living, to which then another people has to subordinate itself, even if some other order is suited to its essential nature ... It does not at all, however, consider the German order obligatory for other peoples. National Socialism, as has been said a hundred times, is exclusively the sum total of the German world-view.[100]

Similar assurances by Nazi leaders were frequently made in order to induce a sense of security in neighboring countries. Hitler, for example, in a proclamation opening the party congress at Nuremberg on September 11, 1935 said:

National Socialism has no aggressive intentions against any European nation. On the contrary, we are convinced that the nations of Europe must continue their characteristic national existence, as created by tradition, history and economy; if not, Europe as a whole will be destroyed.[101]

But such assurances, which were intended exclusively for foreign consumption, were refuted by the basic policy laid down in *Mein Kampf*, which has been persistently pursued throughout the 10 years of the Nazi regime and has been realized to the extent that Germany now dominates and is in control of most of the European continent. In *Mein Kampf* (document 13-I, *post* p. 226) Hitler wrote:

Our task, the mission of the National Socialist movement, however, is to lead our folk to such political insight that it will see its future goal fulfilled not in the intoxicating impression of a new Alexandrian campaign but rather in the industrious work of the German plow, which waits only to be given land by the sword.[102]

Hitler suggests a future foreign policy for Germany which would assure *Lebensraum* and domination of the European continent. In *Mein Kampf* he states:

But the political testament of the German nation for its outwardly directed activity should and must always have the following import:

Never tolerate the establishment of two continental powers in Europe. See an attack against Germany in every attempt to organize a second military power on the German borders, even if it is only in the form of the establishment of a state which is a potential military power, and see therein not only the right but also the duty to prevent the formation of such a state with all means, even to the use of force, or if it has already been established, to destroy it again. See to it that the strength of our folk has its foundations not in colonies but in the soil of the European homeland. Never regard the foundations of the Reich as secure, if it is not able to give every off-shoot of our folk its own bit of soil and territory for centuries to come. Never forget that the most sacred right in the world is the right to the soil which a man wishes to till himself, and the most sacred sacrifice is the blood which he spills for this soil.[103]

It is impossible to adduce from the writings of Hitler, or other Nazi leaders direct statements indicating that they aspire to the domination of the entire world. Such expressions, however, may be inferred not only from the direction of German foreign policy and the effusions of the geopoliticians but also from the following statement made by Hitler in *Mein Kampf* (document 13-I, *post* p. 226):

... If the German folk, in its historical development, had possessed that herdlike unity which other peoples have enjoyed, the German Reich would today be mistress of the globe. World history would have taken another course, and no one can tell whether in this way that might not have been attained which so many deluded pacifists are hoping today to wheedle by moaning and whining: a peace supported not by the palm branches of tearful pacifistic female mourners but founded by the victorious sword of a master race [*Herrenvolk*] which places the world in the service of a higher culture.[1104]

Like Hitler, Rosenberg envisaged the extension of Nazi power far beyond the borders of Germany. In his *Nature, Principles, and Aims of the NSDAP* he stated, "But National Socialism also believes that, far beyond Germany's borders, its principles and its ideology ... will lead the way in the unavoidable struggles for power in the other countries of Europe and America."[1105]

Propaganda
1. Professed Peaceful Intentions as a Cloak for Imperialistic Designs

The falsity of Nazi propaganda has been demonstrated repeatedly during the past decade. That its keynote was set by Hitler himself becomes evident upon an examination of his statements on foreign policy over a period of years. Not only has his policy been marked by a series of shifts and turns, so that the policy of one year was frequently canceled by the policy of the next, but a comparison of his words with his subsequent deeds makes it evident that he deliberately sought to lull other countries into a feeling of security until he was ready to move against them. On May 17, 1933 he asserted:

No fresh European war is capable of putting something better in the place of unsatisfactory conditions which exist to-day ... The outbreak of such madness without end would lead to the collapse of existing social order in Europe ... The German Government are convinced that to-day there can be only one great task, and that is to assure the peace of the world ... *The German Government wish to settle all difficult questions with other Governments by peaceful methods.* They know that any military action in Europe, even if completely successful, would, in view of the sacrifice, bear no relation to the profit to be obtained ...

Germany will tread no other path than that laid down by the Treaties. The German Government will discuss all political and economic questions only within the framework of, and through, the Treaties.

The German people have no thought of invading any country.[1106] (Document 14, *post* pp. 282-233.)

And on March 7, 1936 he stated:

After three years I believe that I can regard the struggle for German equality as concluded to-day. I believe, moreover, that thereby the first and foremost reason for our withdrawal from European collective collaboration has ceased to exist.*We have no territorial demands to make in Europe.*[1107](Document 14, *post* p. 237.)

Moreover, he did not shrink from giving specific assurances of Germany's peaceful intentions toward his subsequent victims:

There are Germans and Poles in Europe, and they ought to live together in agreement. The Poles cannot think, of Europe without the Germans and the Germans cannot think of Europe without the Poles. (Oct. 24, 1933)

Germans and Poles must reconcile themselves as to the fact of each others' existence. It has seemed to me necessary to demonstrate by an example that it is possible for two nations to talk over their differences without giving the task to a third or a fourth ...

The assertion that the German Reich plans to coerce the Austrian State is absurd and cannot be substantiated or proved ... The assertion of the Austrian Government that from the side of the Reich an attack would be undertaken or planned I must emphatically reject ... The German

Reich is always ready to hold out a hand for a real understanding, with full respect for the free will of Austrian Germans ... (Jan. 13, 1934)

The lie goes forth again that Germany to-morrow or the day after will fall upon Austria or Czecho-Slovakia. I ask myself always: Who can these elements be who will have no peace, who incite continually, who must so distrust, and want no understanding? Who are they? I know they are not the millions who, if these inciters had their way, would have to take up arms. (May 1, 1936)

Germany and Poland are two nations, and these nations will live, and neither of them will be able to do away with the other. I recognized all of this, and we all must recognize that a people of 33,000,000 will always strive for an outlet to the sea ... *We have assured all our immediate neighbors of the integrity of their territory as far as Germany is concerned. That is no hollow phrase;   it   is   our   sacred   will ...* (Sept.   26,   1938)[1108] (Document 14, *post* pp. 233, 234, 238, 240-241.)

Yugoslavia is a State that has increasingly attracted the attention of our people since the war. The high regard that the German soldiers then felt for this brave people has since been deepened and developed into genuine friendship. Our economic relations with this country are undergoing constant development and expansion, just as is the case with the friendly countries of Bulgaria, Greece, Rumania, Turkey, Switzerland, Belgium, Holland, Denmark, Norway, Sweden, Finland, and the Baltic States. (Jan. 30, 1939)[1109]

In Hitler's Reichstag speech of April 28, 1939, in which he replied to President Roosevelt's telegraphic message inviting him and Mussolini to pledge themselves not to attack 31 countries mentioned by name, he stated:

... All states bordering on Germany have received much more binding assurances, and above all suggestions, than Mr. Roosevelt asked from me in his curious telegram ...

The German Government is nevertheless prepared to give each of the States named an assurance of the kind desired by Mr. Roosevelt on the condition of absolute reciprocity, provided that the State wishes it and itself addresses to Germany a request for such an assurance together with appropriate proposals.[1110]

And on September 1, 1939, with reference to the recently concluded pact between Germany and Russia, he said:

You know that Russia and Germany are governed by two different doctrines. There was only one question that had to be cleared up. Germany has no intention of exporting its doctrine. Given the fact that Soviet Russia has no intention of exporting its doctrine to Germany, I no longer see any reason why we should still oppose one another. On both sides we are clear on that. Any struggle between our people would only be of advantage to others. We have, therefore, resolved to conclude a pact which rules out forever any use of violence between us.[1111]

Additional assurances of this nature are quoted in a series of extracts from Hitler's speeches, dating from February 10, 1933 to September 1, 1939, which was printed in the *London Times* of September 26, 1939 (document 14, *post* p. 232).

2. *Internal Propaganda*

Within Germany the notorious propaganda machine of Dr. Goebbels, together with a systematic terrorization of oppositionist elements, has been the principle support of the rise and triumph of the Nazi movement. In his *Legal Organization and Legal Functions of the Movement* (document 8, *post* p. 204), Gauweiler gives an idea of the permeation of all phases of national life with a propaganda designed to make Nazi "legal principles" acceptable to the masses. He makes it clear that all of the Nazi propaganda machinery is in the service of this program; political lecturers, the press, the radio, and the films all play a part in helping the people to understand and appreciate the new legal code. The schools and Hitler Youth groups provide instruction for all young people in the fundamentals of National Socialist law, and pupils in those schools which train the carefully selected future leaders are given an especially strong dose of Nazi legal theory and practice.

In order to appeal to the broadest audience, Nazi propaganda has always sought to present all questions in the simplest possible terms. Goebbels himself, in his *Nature and Form of National Socialism* (document 2, *post* p. 170), wrote as follows:

National Socialism has simplified the thinking of the German people and led it back to its original primitive formulas. It has presented the complicated processes of political and economic life in their simplest terms. This was done with the well-considered intention of leading the broad masses of the people once again to take part in political life. In order to find understanding among the masses, we consciously practiced a popular [*volksgebundene*] propaganda. We have taken complexes of facts which were formerly accessible only to a few specialists and experts, carried them to the streets, and hammered them into the brain of the little man. All things were presented so simply that even the most primitive mind could grasp them. We refused to work with unclear or insubstantial concepts but we gave all things a clearly defined sense. Here lay the secret of our success.[112]

The character and quality of Nazi propaganda was fully presaged in *Mein Kampf*. Here Hitler paid a striking tribute to the power of lies, commenting on—

the very correct principle that the size of the lie always involves a certain factor of credibility, since the great mass of a people will be more spoiled in the innermost depths of its heart, rather than consciously and deliberately bad. Consequently, in view of the primitive simplicity of its mind it is more readily captivated by a big lie than by a small one, since it itself often uses small lies but would be, nevertheless, too ashamed to make use of big lies. Such an untruth will not even occur to it, and it will not even believe that others are capable of the enormous insolence of the most vile distortions. Why, even when enlightened, it will still vacillate and be in doubt about the matter and will nevertheless accept as true at least some cause or other. Consequently, even from the most impudent lie something will always stick ...[113]

A number of other passages display Hitler's low opinion of the intellectual capacities and critical faculties of the masses:

All propaganda has to appeal to the people and its intellectual level has to be set in accordance with the receptive capacities of the most-limited persons among those to whom it intends to address itself. The larger the mass of men to be reached, the lower its purely intellectual level will have to be set.[114]

The receptive capacity of the great masses is very restricted, its understanding small. On the other hand, however, its forgetfulness is great. On account of these facts all effective propaganda must restrict itself to very few points and impress these by slogans, until even the last person is able to bring to mind what is meant by such a word.[115]

The task of propaganda is, for instance, not to evaluate diverse rights but to emphasize exclusively the single right of that which it is representing. It does not have to investigate objectively the truth, so far as this is favorable to the others, in order then to present it to the masses in strict honesty, but rather to serve its own side ceaselessly.[116]

If one's own propaganda even once accords just the shimmer of right to the other side, then the basis is therewith laid for doubt regarding one's own cause. The masses are not able to distinguish where the error of the other side ends and the error of one's own side begins.[117]

But all talent in presentation of propaganda will lead to no success if a fundamental principle is not always strictly followed. Propaganda has to restrict itself to a few matters and to repeat these eternally. Persistence is here, as with so many other things in the world, the first and most important presupposition for success.[118]

In view of their slowness of mind, they [the masses] require always, however, a certain period before they are ready even to take cognizance of a matter, and only after a thousandfold repetition of the most simple concept will they finally retain it.[119]

In all cases in which there is a question of the fulfilment of apparently impossible demands or tasks, the entire attention of a people must be concentrated only on this one question, in such a way as if being or non-being actually depends on its solution ...

...The great mass of the people can never see the entire way before them, without tiring and doubting the task.[120]

In general the art of all truly great popular leaders at all times consists primarily in not scattering the attention of a people but rather in concentrating it always on one single opponent. The more unified this use of the fighting will of a people, the greater will be the magnetic attractive force of a movement and the more powerful the force of its push. It is a part of the genius of a great leader to make even quite different opponents appear as if they belonged only to one category, because the recognition of different enemies leads weak and unsure persons only too readily to begin doubting their own cause.

When the vacillating masses see themselves fighting against too many enemies, objectivity at once sets in and raises the question whether really all the others are wrong and only one's own people or one's own movement is right.[121](Document 13-II, *post* pp. 229-231.)

It has been the aim of Nazi propaganda, then, to unite the masses of the people in hatred of certain enemies, designated by such conveniently broad and simple terms as "Jews," "democrats," "plutocrats," "bolshevists," or "Anglo-Saxons," which so far as possible were to be identified with one another in the public mind. The Germans were represented to themselves, on the other hand, as a racial folk of industrious workers. It then became possible to plunge the people into a war on a wave of emotional hatred against those nations which were pictured as combining to keep Germany from attaining her rightful place in the sun.

The important role which propaganda would have to play in the coming war was fully recognized by Ewald Banse, an ardent Nazi military theorist of the geopolitical school and professor of military science at Brunswick Military College. In his book *Raum und Volk im Weltkrieg (Space and People in the World War)* which appeared in 1932 (an English translation by Alan Harris was published under the title *Germany Prepares for War* (New York, Harcourt, Brace and Co., 1934)), he stated:

Preparation for future wars must not stop at the creation, equipment and training of an efficient army, but must go on to train the minds of the whole people for the war and must employ all the resources of science to master the conditions governing the war itself and the possibility of endurance. In 1914 we had a first-class army, but our scientific mobilization was bad, and the mobilization of men's minds a thing undreamed of. The unveiling of war memorials, parades of war veterans, flag-waggings, fiery speeches and guard-mounting are not of themselves enough to prepare a nation's mind for the dangers that threaten. Conviction is always more lasting than enthusiasm.

... Such teaching is necessary at a time and in a world in which countries are no longer represented by monarchs or a small aristocracy or by a specialist army, but in which the whole nation, from the commander-in-chief to the man in the ranks, from the loftiest thought to the simplest wish, from corn to coal, from the treasury vaults to the last trouser-button, must be permeated through and through with the idea of national defense, if it is to preserve its national identity and political independence. The science of national defense is not the same as military science; it does not teach generals how to win battles or company commanders how to train recruits. Its lessons are addressed first and foremost to the whole people. It seeks to train the popular mind to heroism and war and to implant in it an understanding of the nature and prerequisite conditions of modern warfare. It teaches us about countries and peoples, especially our own country and its neighbors, their territories and economic capacity, their communications and their mentality—all for the purpose of creating the best possible conditions for waging future wars in defense of the national existence.[122]

Infiltration Tactics

The Nazis, while entirely without scruple in the pursuit of their objectives, endeavor whenever possible to give their actions the cloak of legality. This procedure was followed in Germany to enable them to gain control of the Government of the Reich and in their foreign policy up to September 1, 1939. It has been a cardinal principle of the Nazis to avoid the use of force whenever their objectives may be attained in another manner and they have assiduously studied their enemies in an effort to discover the weak points in their structure which will enable the Nazis to accomplish their downfall. The preceding pages have demonstrated that the Nazis have contributed practically nothing that is original to German political thought. By the use of unscrupulous, deceitful, and uninhibited tactics, however, they have been able to realize many of the objectives which had previously existed only in theory.

The Weimar Constitution provided the Nazis with a convenient basis for the establishment of the totalitarian state. They made no effort to conceal their intention of taking advantage of the weaknesses of the Weimar Republic in order to attain power. On April 30, 1928 Dr. Goebbels wrote in his paper *Der Angriff*:

We enter Parliament in order to supply ourselves, in the arsenal of democracy, with its own weapons. We become members of the Reichstag in order to paralyze the Weimar sentiment with its own assistance. If democracy is so stupid as to give us free tickets and salaries for this bear's work, that is its affair ...[123]

And later in the same article:

We do not come as friends, nor even as neutrals. We come as enemies. As the wolf bursts into the flock, so we come.[124]

Hitler expressed the same idea on September 1, 1933, when, looking back upon the struggle for political power in Germany, he wrote:

This watchword of democratic freedom led only to insecurity, indiscipline, and at length to the downfall and destruction of all authority. *Our opponents' objection that we, too, once made use of these rights, will not hold water; for we made use of an unreasonable right, which was part and parcel of an unreasonable system, in order to overthrow the unreason of this system.*[125]

Discussing the rise to power of the Nazis, Huber (document 1, *post* p. 155) wrote in 1939:

The parliamentary battle of the NSDAP had the single purpose of destroying the parliamentary system from within through its own methods. It was necessary above all to make formal use of the possibilities of the party-state system but to refuse real cooperation and thereby to render the parliamentary system, which is by nature dependent upon the responsible cooperation of the opposition, incapable of action.[126]

As its parliamentary strength increased, the party was able to achieve these aims:

It was in a position to make the formation of any positive majority in the Reichstag impossible.... Thus the NSDAP was able through its strong position to make the Reichstag powerless as a lawgiving and government-forming body.[127]

The same principle was followed by Germany in weakening and undermining the governments of countries which it had chosen for its victims. While it was Hitler's policy to concentrate on only one objective at a time, German agents were busy throughout the world in ferreting out the natural political, social, and economic cleavages in various countries and in broadening them in order to create internal confusion and uncertainty. Foreign political leaders of Fascist or authoritarian persuasion were encouraged and often liberally subsidized from Nazi funds. Control was covertly obtained over influential newspapers and periodicals and their editorial policies shaped in such a way as to further Nazi ends. In the countries Germany sought to overpower, all the highly developed organs of Nazi propaganda were utilized to confuse and divide public opinion, to discredit national leaders and institutions, and to induce an unjustified feeling of confidence in the false assertions of Nazi leaders disclaiming any aggressive intentions.

One of the most important features introduced by the Nazis into German foreign policy was the appreciation of the value of Germans living abroad and their organization as implements of the Reich for the attainment of objectives in the field of foreign policy. This idea was applied by the Nazis to all the large colonies of Germans which are scattered throughout the world. The potential usefulness of these colonies was early recognized by the men in Hitler's immediate entourage, several of whom were so-called *Auslandsdeutsche* who had spent many years of their life abroad and were familiar with foreign conditions and with the position and influence of German groups in foreign countries. Of particular importance in this group were Rudolf Hess, the Führer's Deputy, who was primarily responsible for elaborating the policy which utilized the services of Germans abroad, and Ernst Wilhelm Bohle, the leader of the Foreign Organization, who was responsible for winning over these

Germans to Naziism and for their organization in groups which would serve the purposes of the Third Reich.

FOOTNOTES:

[94] Feder, *op. cit.*, p. 18.
[95] Gauweiler, *op. cit.*, pp. 149-151.
[96] *Mein Kampf*, pp. 727-728.
[97] *Ibid.*, pp. 735-736.
[98] Scurla, *op. cit.*, p. 21.
[99] *Ibid.*, pp. 21-22.
[100] *Ibid.*, p. 23.
[101] *Der Parteitag der Freiheit* (official record of the 1935 party congress at Nuremberg: Munich, 1935), p. 27.
[102] *Mein Kampf*, p. 743.
[103] *Ibid.*, pp. 754-755.
[104] *Ibid.*, pp. 437-438.
[105] Rosenberg, *Wesen, Grundsätze und Ziele der NSDAP*, p. 48.
[106] *London Times*, Sept. 26, 1939, p. 9.
[107] *Ibid.*
[108] *Ibid.*
[109] *My New Order*, p. 592.
[110] *Ibid.*, pp. 669-671.
[111] *Ibid.*, p. 687.
[112] Goebbels, *op. cit.*, p. 6.
[113] *Mein Kampf*, p. 252.
[114] *Ibid.*, p. 197.
[115] *Ibid.*, p. 198.
[116] *Ibid.*, p. 200.
[117] *Ibid.*, pp. 200-201.
[118] *Ibid.*, p. 202.
[119] *Ibid.*, p. 203.
[120] *Ibid.*, p. 273.
[121] *Ibid.*, p. 129.
[122] Banse, *Germany Prepares for War* (New York, 1934), pp. 348-349.
[123] Goebbels, *Der Angriff: Aufsätze aus der Kampfzeit* (Munich, 1936), p. 71.
[124] *Ibid.*, p. 73.
[125] *My New Order*, pp. 195-196.
[126] Huber, *Verfassungsrecht des grossdeutschen Reiches* (Hamburg, 1939), p. 31.
[127] *Ibid.*, p. 32.

NATIONAL-SOCIALISM AND MEDICINE

ToC

Address by Dr. F. Hamburger to German Medical Profession.
Translated (in part) from Wiener Klinische Wochenschrift, 1939, No. 6.

Medical men must beware of pride, a pride which is certainly wide-spread and which leads to the disparagement of the practical doctor and medical layman, and then further to the disparagement of the craft of nature healers. The practical doctor and the nature healer on the one hand tend towards an understandable disparagement of medical science and analysis and, on the other hand, tend towards superficiality. The superficiality of the opponents of science is, however, as unhappy an affair as the pride of the so-called scientists, but the one group should not demean the other. This would lead to successful cooperation to the advantage of the sick and health of the community.

Academic medicine and nature healers generally have one thing in common, that they underestimate the significance of automatism and suggestion. In this regard there is an absence in both camps of the necessary criticism and clarity. Successes are noted with specific methods without any confirmation as to whether or not suggestion and faith alone have not produced the improvement in the patient.

National-Socialism is the true instrument for the achievement of the health of our people. National-Socialism is concerned with the great significance of inherited traits and with the insight into the working of spiritual forces upon the body, with the study of the power of custom and, along with this, of the significance of education and nurture. (Hamburger here complains about the luxurious arrangement for dealing with the mentally ill in contradistinction to the neglect of Folk-health. This he attributes to the era of liberalism with its stress upon the single individual. He here also attacks the Socialism of Social Democracy and its conception of a Community of Equal Men. This is a false Socialism.)

So we scientists and doctors simply and soberly affirm the principle of strength of faith and the nationalist socialist principle of Positive Christianity which does not prevent us from the inspired consideration of natural and divinely willed phenomena. We doctors must never forget the fact that the soul rules the body.

Soul forces are the most important. The spirit builds the body. Strength springs from joy. Efficiency is achieved despite care, fear, and uncertainty—We speak here of thymogenetic automatism or the automatism of harmony ("thymogenetische automatismus oder stimmungsautomatismus"). The autonomous nervous system achieves, under the influence of joy, the expansion of the blood vessels in skin and muscle.... The muscular activity incited by joy means the use of calories and stimulation of appetite. Muscular contraction pulls and draws at the bones, ligaments are tensed, breathing deepend, appetite increased ... A child influenced by the daily exercise of joy develops physically strong and powerful. ... The Soul care (Seele Sorge) of the practical doctor is his most significant daily task alongside of prescriptions and manipulative dexterity.

Soul-care in the medical sense is a concern for the wishes, hopes and fears of the patient, the considered participation in his fate. Such a relationship leads to the all-important and generally recognized trust in the doctor. This faith, in all cases, leads to the improvement, often even to the elimination of symptoms, of the disease. Here we have clearly before us the great significance of thymogenetic automatism.

Academic physicians should not dismiss this because we do not know its biochemical aspects. (We must beware of regarding something as unacceptable because it is not measurable in exact terms, he warns.) We see its practical results, and, therefore, thymogenetic automatism must stand in the first rank as of overwhelming significance. Thus, also, the principle, strength through joy (Kraft durch Freude) stands firmly as an inescapable natural law.

We see the practical country doctor spreading courage and confidence. For years too few doctors have seen clearly that gymnastic tourism and sport do more for health than all doctors taken together. And now we face the fact that a single man, a non-medical man (Hitler) through his great qualities, has opened up new avenues of health for the eighty million folk of Germany.

In the majority of cases things so happen that the doctor must act before making a diagnosis, since only the mis-educated patients, the one-sided intellectual patient, wishes in the very first place to know the diagnosis. But the unspoilt and properly ordered type of person wishes only to be relieved of his pain. For him the diagnosis is an interesting side issue but not the principle thing. We can thus also understand why we always meet the desire for a diagnosis placed first by the over-intellectualized Jewish patient. But that is not the case with most Aryan patients. They, from the first, come to meet the doctor with more trust. They do not entertain as many after-thoughts. And I cannot help but remark that after-thoughts are hardly conducive to right results.

(After a discussion of the sterilization of the unfit and of inheritable diseases he turns to the subject of child bearing.)

It has been estimated that every couple should have four children if the nation's population is to be maintained. But we meet already the facile and complacent expression of young married people, "Now we have our four children and so have fulfilled our obligations"—What superficiality! Today we must demand a much higher moral attitude from the wife than previously. Earlier it was taken for granted that a woman would bear a child every one or two years. But today in this time of manifold amenities of life, at a time when women is not denied access to these joys it is understandable that she is eager to participate in them. Add to this that the knowledge of birth control is general today. Despite all this women must be encouraged to give birth during twenty years of married life to eight or ten and even more children, and to renounce the above-mentioned joys of life. She must decide as a mother of children to lead a life full of sacrifices, devotion, and unselfishness. It is only when these ethical demands are fulfilled by a large number of worthy wives of good stock that the future of the German nation will be assured.

Doctors are leaders of the Folk more than they know ... They are now quite officially fuehrer of the people, called to the leadership of its health. To fulfill this task they must be free of the profit motive. They must be quite free from that attitude of spirit which is rightly designated as Jewish, the concern for business and self-provision.

SELECTED BIBLIOGRAPHY

ToC

Arendt, Hannah—*The Origins of Totalitarianism*, N.Y., 1951.

Pt. III is especially directed to a discussion of the principles and consequences of fascism. The author gives an effective account of what "total domination" signifies in a reign of terror. Detailed bibliography.

Bodrero, Emilio—"Fascism" in *Dictatorship on Its Trial*, ed. by Otto Forst de Battaglia, London, 1930.

A brief, but significant, statement by a former Rector of the University of Padua and a Secretary of State to Mussolini.

Borgese, G.A.—*Goliath, The March of Fascism*, N.Y., 1938.

Well written from the point of view of an Italian humanist.

Brady, Robert A.—*The Spirit and Structure of German Fascism*, London, 1937.

An extremely thorough and documented discussion of the economy of National Socialist Germany, its institutions and its business practices.

See also: Brady's *Business as a System of Power*, chapters on Germany, Italy and Japan. N.Y., 1943.

Childs, H.L. and Dodd, W.E.—*The Nazi Primer*, N.Y., 1938.

A translation of the "Official Handbook for Schooling the Hitler Youth." In simple form including illustrations, it is an excellent indication of the guiding principles of the German educational system.

Dennis, Lawrence—*The Coming American Fascism*, N.Y., 1936. *The Dynamics of War and Revolution*, N.Y., 1940.

Two books by the only fascist theorist in America.

Fraenkel, Ernest—*The Dual State: A Contribution to the Theory of Dictatorship*,N.Y., 1941.

By distinguishing between the "Prerogative State" and the "Normative State," the author gives an effective account of the attempt of the Nazis to acknowledge an indispensable, if minimal, legal order, which was, comparatively speaking, independent of the extra-legal realm of violence.

Hartshorne, E.Y.—*The German Universities and National Socialism*, Cambridge, 1937.

A carefully documented account of what happened in the various branches and departments of German universities under the Nazis.

Hitler, Adolph—*My Battle*, N.Y., 1939.

Hitler's own vitriolic account of his attempt to rise to power.

Lasswell, Harold D.—"The Garrison State," *American Journal of Sociology*, Chicago, Vol. XLVI, 1940-41, pp. 455-468.

A brief but incisive discussion of the structure of fascism.

Lilge, Frederic—*The Abuse of Learning: The Failure of the German University*,N.Y., 1948.

A philosophical history of higher education in Germany, concluding with its fascist evolution.

Matteotti, Giacomo—*The Fascist Exposed: A Year of Fascist Domination*, London, 1924.

A factual account by a liberal, who, until murdered, was a member of the Italian Senate.

Minio-Paluello, L.—*Education in Fascist Italy*, N.Y., 1946.

A detailed discussion of fascist education, including an historical introduction to pre-fascist education.

Neumann, Franz—*Behemoth: The Structure and Practice of National Socialism*, N.Y., 1942.

Probably the most comprehensive and definitive statement in English of the functioning of National Socialism. It concentrates especially on the political and economic aspects of Nazism.

Pinthus, Kurt—"Culture Under Nazi Germany," *The American Scholar*, Vol. IX, N.Y., 1940, pp. 483-498.

A valuable treatment of the inner character of the arts and letters and of what happened to their publics under the Nazis.

Sabine, G.H.—*A History of Political Theory*, N.Y., 1950.

A brief chapter on "Fascism" gives an excellent balanced account of its fundamentals.

Salvemini, Gaetano—*The Fascist Dictatorship in Italy*, N.Y., 1927. *Under the Axe of Fascism*, N.Y., 1936.

An eminent Italian historian writes vividly and perceptively on Italian Fascism.

Schneider, Herbert W.—*Making the Fascist State*, N.Y., 1928.

An early, but well considered, account of the rise of Italian fascism.

Silone, Ignazio—*Fontamara*, Verona, 1951.

The best novel on Italian fascism.

Spender, Stephen—*European Witness*, N.Y., 1946.

Note especially the analysis of Goebbel's novel, *Michael*.

Trevor-Roper, H.R.—*The Last Days of Hitler*, N.Y., 1946.

An intimate portrayal of Hitler and his entourage from the time of the beginning of the collapse of the Nazi armies. Especially good on the rift between the politicians and the military.

READINGS ON FASCISM AND NATIONAL SOCIALISM

The catastrophe and holocaust brought about by the two powerful movements of fascism and national socialism will mark human life always. Now, as we feel our hatred for them, we find it difficult to understand how they could have been so powerful, how they could have appealed so strongly to millions of people of a modern age.

And the documents whereby we could understand these philosophies have been lost—except as they are now gathered here in one convenient volume.

To understand our own times, it is necessary to understand these movements. And to understand them, we must read the basic philosophical and political documents which show the force of the ideas which moved a world to the brink of disaster.

THE FIRST SWALLOW PAPERBOOKS:

1. A FIELD OF BROKEN STONES by Lowell Naeve.

A profound book written in a prison. $1.65.

2. THE WIFE OF MARTIN GUERRE by Janet Lewis.

One of the fine short novels of all time. $1.25.

3. READINGS ON FASCISM AND NATIONAL SOCIALISM.

A grouping together of authoritative readings. $1.35.

  4. THE TEACHER OF ENGLISH by James E. Warren, Jr.
The Materials and Opportunities of the teacher. $1.35.
  5. MORNING RED by Frederick Manfred.
The most ambitious novel by a powerful writer. $1.95.

   ALAN   SWALLOW
2679 So. York St., Denver 10, Colo.

Printed in the USA
CPSIA information can be obtained
at www.ICGtesting.com
LVHW050246091224
798664LV00011B/882